CISI

CHARTERED INSTITUTE FOR
SECURITIES & INVESTMENT

Introduction to Investment

• • • • • • • • • • • • •

The Official Learning and Reference Manual

3rd Edition, April 2010

This Workbook relates to syllabus version 10.0 and will cover examinations from
1st July 2010 to 30th June 2011

PROFESSIONALISM | INTEGRITY | EXCELLENCE

CHARTERED INSTITUTE FOR
SECURITIES & INVESTMENT

INTRODUCTION TO INVESTMENT

Welcome to the Chartered Institute for Securities & Investment's Introduction to Investment study material.

This workbook has been written to prepare you for the Chartered Institute for Securities & Investment's Introduction to Investment examination.

PUBLISHED BY:

Chartered Institute for Securities & Investment
© Chartered Institute for Securities & Investment 2010
8 Eastcheap
London EC3M 1AE
Tel: +44 (0) 20 7645 0600
Fax: + 44 (0) 20 7645 0601

WRITTEN BY:
Kevin Rothwell on behalf of the Chartered Institute for Securities & Investment

TECHNICAL REVIEW BY:

Keith Laver

SENIOR REVIEW BY:
Lynn Berger

WITH GRATEFUL THANKS TO:
IMA

This is an educational manual only and Chartered Institute for Securities & Investment accepts no responsibility for persons undertaking trading or investments in whatever form.

While every effort has been made to ensure its accuracy, no responsibility for loss occasioned to any person acting or refraining from action as a result of any material in this publication can be accepted by the publisher or authors.

A Learning Map, which contains the full syllabus, appears at the end of this workbook. The syllabus can also be viewed on the Institute's website at www.cisi.org and is also available by contacting Client Services on +44 (0) 20 7645 0680. Please note that the examination is based upon the syllabus. Candidates are reminded to check the Candidate Common Room area of the Institute's website (www.cisi.org/candidatecommonroom) on a regular basis for updates that could affect their examination as a result of industry change.

The questions contained in this manual are designed as an aid to revision of different areas of the syllabus and to help you consolidate your learning chapter by chapter.

Workbook version: 3.1 (April 2010)

FOREWORD

Learning and Professional Development with the CISI

Formerly the Securities & Investment Institute (SII), and originally founded by members of the London Stock Exchange in 1992, the Institute is the leading examining, membership and awarding body for the securities and investment industry. We were awarded a royal charter in October 2009, becoming the Chartered Institute for Securities & Investment. We currently have around 40,000 members who benefit from a programme of professional and social events, with continuing professional development (CPD) and the promotion of integrity, very much at the heart of everything we do.

This learning manual (or 'workbook' as it is often known in the industry) provides not only a thorough preparation for the appropriate CISI examination, but is a valuable desktop reference for practitioners. It can also be used as a learning tool for readers interested in knowing more, but not necessarily entering an examination.

The CISI official learning manuals ensure that candidates gain a comprehensive understanding of examination content. Our material is written and updated by industry specialists and reviewed by experienced, senior figures in the financial services industry. Exam and manual quality is assured through a rigorous editorial system of practitioner panels and boards. CISI examinations are used extensively by firms to meet the requirements of government regulators. The CISI works closely with a number of international regulators which recognise our examinations and the manuals supporting them, as well as the UK regulator, the Financial Services Authority (FSA).

CISI learning manuals are normally revised annually. It is important that candidates check they purchase the correct version for the period when they wish to take their examination. Between versions, candidates should keep abreast of the latest industry developments through the Candidate Commonroom area of the CISI website. (The CISI also endorses the workbooks of 7City Learning and BPP.)

The CISI produces a range of elearning revision tools such as Revision Express Interactive, Revision Express Online and Professional Refresher that can be used in conjunction with our learning and reference manuals. For further details, please visit cisi.org.

As a Professional Body, around 40,000 CISI members subscribe to the CISI Code of Conduct and the CISI has a significant voice in the industry, standing for professionalism, excellence and the promotion of trust and integrity. Continuing professional development is at the heart of the Institute's values. Our CPD scheme is available free of charge to members, and this includes an online record keeping system as well as regular seminars, conferences and professional networks in specialist subjects areas, all of which cover a range of current industry topics. Reading this manual and taking a CISI examination is credited as professional development with the CISI CPD scheme. To learn more about CISI membership visit our website at cisi.org.

We hope that you will find this manual useful and interesting. Once you have completed it you will find helpful suggestions on qualifications and membership progression with the CISI at the end of this book.

With best wishes for your studies.

Ruth Martin
Managing Director

CONTENTS

Welcome to the latest edition of the CISI's workbook for the IAQTM Introduction to Investment examination.

What next?
See the back of this book for details on CISI membership.

Need more support to pass your exam?
See our section on Accredited Training Providers and CISI elearning at the back of this book.

Want to leave feedback?
Please email your comments to learningresources@cisi.org

It is estimated that this workbook will require approximately **70** hours of study time.

WORKBOOK HOTSPOTS
Within your workbook you will see **HOTSPOTS** like this:

> **HOTSPOT**
> **4**
> Go online to your elearning product for further information on bonds.
>
> If you haven't purchased your elearning product, you can order now by calling Client Services on +44(0)20 7645 0680.

These **HOTSPOTS** will prompt you to view your elearning product for further information on a particular part of the workbook.

CHAPTER ONE

FINANCIAL SERVICES INDUSTRY

This syllabus area will provide approximately 2 of the 50 examination questions

1. INTRODUCTION

Stock markets and investment instruments are not unique to one country and there is increasing similarity in the instruments that are traded on all world markets and in the way that trading and settlement systems are developing. As a result, this chapter looks at how the industry is structured and examines some of its key participants.

Until recently, the world economy grew rapidly and became increasingly integrated and interdependent as trade and investment flows rose. The subsequent credit crisis has further emphasised the global nature of the financial services industry and how a crisis in one country, such as the sub-prime crisis in the US or the collapse of Lehman Brothers, had an impact across world markets.

With this background, therefore, it is important to understand the core role that the financial services industry undertakes within the economy and some of the key features of the global financial services sector. This will be considered in the following sections.

The financial services industry in developed countries is a major contributor to the economy. In the UK, for example, the activities of the firms located in and around the City of London provide considerable employment, as well as overseas earnings for the economy.

The financial services industry provides the link between organisations needing capital and those with capital available for investment. An organisation needing capital might be a growing company, and the capital might be provided by individuals saving for their retirement in a pension fund. It is the financial services industry that channels the money invested to those organisations that need it, and provides transmission, payment, advisory and management services.

2. PROFESSIONAL AND RETAIL BUSINESS

LEARNING OBJECTIVES

1.1.2   Know the function of and differences between retail and professional business and who the main customers are in each case: retail clients and professional clients

Within the financial services industry there are two distinct areas, namely the wholesale or professional sector (also known as the institutional sector) and the retail sector.

The financial activities that make up the wholesale/professional sector include:

- **international banking** – cross-border banking transactions;
- **equity markets** – the trading of quoted shares;
- **bond markets** – the trading of government, supranational or corporate debt;
- **foreign exchange** – the trading of currencies;
- **derivatives** – the trading of options, swaps, futures and forwards;
- **fund management** – managing the investment portfolios of collective investment schemes, pension funds and insurance funds;

- **insurance** – re-insurance, major corporate insurance (including professional indemnity), captive insurance and risk-sharing insurance;
- **investment banking** – tailored banking services to organisations, such as undertaking mergers and acquisitions, equity trading, fixed income trading and private equity;
- **custodian banking** – provision of services to asset managers involving the safekeeping of assets; the administration of the underlying investments; settlement; corporate action and other specialised activities.

By contrast, the retail sector focuses on services provided to personal customers including:

- **retail banking** – traditional range of deposit accounts, lending and credit cards;
- **insurance** – provision of a range of life assurance and protection solutions for areas such as medical insurance, critical illness, motor, property, income protection and mortgage protection;
- **pensions** – provision of investment accounts specifically designed to capture savings during a person's working life and provide benefits on retirement;
- **investment services** – a range of investment products and vehicles ranging from execution-only stockbroking to full wealth management services and private banking;
- **financial planning and financial advice**.

3. INDUSTRY PARTICIPANTS

LEARNING OBJECTIVES

1.1.1   Know the role of the following within the financial services industry: retail banks; building societies; investment banks; pension funds; insurance companies; fund managers; stockbrokers; custodians; third party administrators (TPAs); industry trade and professional bodies

The following sections provide descriptions of some of the main participants in the financial services industry:

3.1   Retail Banks

Retail, (or high street), banks provide services such as taking deposits from and lending funds to, retail customers, as well as providing payment and money transmission services. They may also provide similar services to business customers.

Historically, these banks have tended to operate through a network of branches located on the high street. They also provide internet and telephone banking.

In the UK, the sector has gone through a period of consolidation and, increasingly, integration with non-bank institutions such as insurance companies. As well as providing traditional banking services, larger retail banks also offer products such as investments, pensions and insurance.

3.2   Savings Institutions

As well as retail banks, most countries also have savings institutions that started off by specialising in offering savings products to retail customers, but now tend to offer a similar range of services to banks.

In the UK, they are usually known as building societies. They were established in the 19th century when small numbers of people would group together and pool their savings, allowing some members to build or buy houses. Building societies are jointly owned by the individuals that have deposited or borrowed money from them – the 'members'. It is for this reason that such savings organisations are often described as mutual societies.

Over the years, many smaller building societies have merged or been taken over by larger ones.

In the late 1980s, legislation was introduced allowing building societies to become companies – a process known as 'demutualisation'.

Some large building societies remain as mutuals, such as the Nationwide Building Society. They continue to specialise in services for retail customers, especially the provision of deposit accounts and mortgages.

3.3   Investment Banks

Investment banks provide advice and arrange finance for companies who want to float on the stock market, raise additional finance by issuing further shares or bonds, or carry out mergers and acquisitions. They also provide services for those who might want to invest in shares and bonds, for example, pension funds and asset managers.

The financial crisis of 2008 saw the disappearance of most investment banks. They were either taken over by other banks or converted into bank holding companies. For example, Merrill Lynch was taken over by Bank of America.

Typically, an investment banking group provides some or all of the following services, either in divisions of the bank or in associated companies within the group:

*   Corporate finance and advisory work, normally in connection with new issues of securities for raising finance, takeovers, mergers and acquisitions.
*   Banking, for governments, institutions and companies.
*   Treasury dealing for corporate clients in foreign currencies, with financial engineering services to protect them from interest and exchange rate fluctuations.
*   Investment management for sizeable investors such as corporate pension funds, charities, and private clients. They may do this either via direct investment for the wealthier, or by way of collective investment schemes. In larger firms, the value of funds under management runs into many billions of pounds.
*   Securities trading in equities, bonds and derivatives and the provision of broking and distribution facilities.

Only a few investment banks provide services in all these areas. Most others tend to specialise to some degree and concentrate on only a few product lines.

> **HOTSPOT**
>
> | I |
>
> Go online to your elearning product for further information on investment banks.
>
> If you haven't purchased your elearning product, you can order now by calling Client Services on +44(0)20 7645 0680.

3.4   Pension Funds

Pension funds are one of the key planning methods by which individuals can make provision for retirement.

There are a variety of pension schemes available ranging from ones provided by employers to self-directed schemes.

Pension funds are large, long-term investors in shares, bonds and cash. Some also invest in physical assets, like property. To meet their aim of providing a pension on retirement, the sums of money invested in pensions are substantial.

3.5   Insurance Companies

One of the key functions of the financial services industry is to allow risks to be managed effectively. The insurance industry provides solutions for much more than the standard areas of life and general insurance cover.

Protection planning is a key area of financial advice and the insurance industry provides a wide range of products to meet many potential scenarios. These products range from payment protection policies designed to pay out in the event that an individual is unable to meet repayments on loans and mortgages, to fleet insurance against the risk of an airline's planes crashing.

Insurance companies also market a wide range of investment products and have recently become large players in what is known as the 'structured products' market by offering guaranteed stock market-related bonds.

Insurance companies collect premiums in exchange for the cover provided. This premium income is used to buy investments such as shares and bonds and as a result, the insurance industry is a major player in the London stock market. Insurance companies will subsequently realise these investments to pay any claims that may arise on the various policies.

The UK insurance industry is the largest in Europe and the second largest in the world.

3.6   Fund Management

Fund management is the administration of portfolios for pension funds, insurance companies and collective investment schemes and is also known as **'asset management'** or **'investment management'**.

Other areas of fund management include private wealth management and the provision of investment management services to institutional entities, such as companies, charities and local government authorities. This area also includes hedge funds.

Fund managers, also known as investment or asset managers, run portfolios of investments for others. They invest money held by institutions, such as pension funds and insurance companies, as well as for collective investment schemes, such as unit trusts and OEICs and for wealthier individuals. Some are organisations which focus solely on this activity; others are divisions of larger entities, like insurance companies or banks.

Investment managers who buy and sell shares, bonds and other assets in order to increase the value of their clients' portfolios, can conveniently be sub-divided into 'institutional' and 'private client' fund managers.

Institutional fund managers work on behalf of institutions, for example, investing money for a company's pension fund, or an insurance company's fund, or managing the investments in a unit trust. Private client fund managers invest the money of relatively wealthy individuals. Institutional portfolios are usually larger than those of private clients.

Investment managers charge their clients for managing their money; their charges are often based on a small percentage of the fund being managed.

3.7   Stockbrokers

Stockbrokers arrange stock market trades on behalf of their clients, who are mainly 'private clients'. They may advise investors about which individual shares, bonds or funds they should buy or, alternatively, they may offer execution-only services.

Like fund managers, firms of stockbrokers can be independent companies, but usually they are divisions of larger entities, such as investment banks. They earn their profits by charging fees for their advice and commissions on transactions.

3.8   Custodian Banks

Custodians are banks that specialise in safe custody services looking after portfolios of shares and bonds on behalf of others, such as fund managers, pension funds and insurance companies.

The core activities they undertake include:

- holding assets in safekeeping, such as equities and bonds;
- arranging settlement of any purchases and sales of securities;
- collecting income from assets, namely dividends in the case of equities and interest in the case of bonds;

- providing information on the underlying companies and their annual general meetings;
- managing cash transactions;
- performing foreign exchange transactions where required; and
- providing regular reporting on all their activities to their clients.

Cost pressures have driven down the charges that a custodian can make for its traditional custody services and have resulted in consolidation within the industry. The custody business is now dominated by a small number of global custodians which are often divisions of investment banks.

3.9 Trade and Professional Bodies

The investment industry is a dynamic, rapidly changing business and requires co-operation between firms to ensure that the views of various industry sections are represented, especially to government and regulators. The industry also facilitates and enables cross-firm developments to take place to create an efficient market in which the firms can operate.

This is essentially the role of the numerous professional and trade bodies that exist across the world's financial markets. Examples of such bodies include:

- **Bonds** – International Capital Markets Association.
- **Derivatives** – Futures and Options Association; International Swaps and Derivatives Association.
- **Fund Managers** – Investment Management Association (IMA).
- **Insurance Companies** – Association of British Insurers (ABI).
- **Private Client Investment Management** – Association of Private Client Investment Managers (APCIMs).

3.10 Third Party Administrators

Third Party Administrators (TPAs) undertake investment administration on behalf of other firms and specialise in this area of the investment industry.

The number of firms and the scale of their operations have grown with the increasing use of outsourcing by firms. The rationale behind outsourcing is that it enables a firm to focus on the core areas of its business (for example, investment management and stock selection, or the provision of appropriate financial planning) and leaves another firm to carry on the administrative functions which it can process more efficiently and cost effectively.

4. INVESTMENT DISTRIBUTION CHANNELS

LEARNING OBJECTIVES

1.1.3   Know the role of the following investment distribution channels:
independent financial adviser; tied adviser; platforms; execution only

4.1   Financial Advisers

Financial advisers are professionals who offer advice on financial matters to their clients. Some recommend suitable financial products from the whole of the market and others from a narrower range of products.

Typically a financial adviser will conduct a detailed survey of a client's financial position, preferences and objectives; this is sometimes known as a 'factfind'. The adviser will then suggest appropriate action to meet the client's objectives and, if necessary, recommend a suitable financial product to match the client's needs.

In the UK, there are now four main classes of adviser:

- **tied advisers**, who advise on the products of one financial institution;
- **multi-tied advisers**, who advise on the products of more than one financial institution;
- **whole of market advisers**, who advise on the products of all the UK companies active in that area and who are paid by way of commission on the products they sell;
- **independent financial advisers**, who also advise on the whole range of products on offer in the market – but who must also offer their clients the option to pay for advice by fee rather than by commission.

At the time of writing, the Financial Services Authority (FSA) is consulting on changes as to how investment products and services are distributed to retail clients. The Retail Distribution Review (RDR) contains proposals to change the classes of adviser referred to above.

Investment firms will have to clearly describe their services as either 'independent advice' or 'restricted advice'. Firms that describe their advice as independent will have to ensure that they genuinely do make their recommendations based on comprehensive and fair analysis, and provide unbiased, unrestricted advice. Where a firm chooses to only give advice on its own range of products this will have to be made clear.

The FSA are due to publish their new rules in the first quarter of 2010 and the proposals will take effect from the end of 2012.

4.2   Platforms

Platforms are online services used by intermediaries to view and administer their clients' investment portfolios. Platform providers also make their services available direct to investors.

They offer a range of tools which allow advisers to see and analyse a client's overall portfolio and to choose products for them. As well as providing facilities for investments to be bought and sold, platforms generally arrange custody for clients' assets.

The term 'platform' refers to both wraps and fund supermarkets. These are similar, but while fund supermarkets tend to offer wide ranges of unit trusts and OEICs, wraps often offer greater access to other products too, such as Individual Savings Accounts (ISAs), pension plans and insurance bonds.

Wrap accounts enable advisers to take a holistic view of the various assets that a client has in a variety of accounts. Advisers also benefit from using wrap accounts to simplify and bring some level of automation to their back-office using internet technology. The advantage for fund management groups is the ability of the platform to distribute their products to financial advisers.

Platforms earn their income by either charging for their services or by taking commission from the product provider rather than the agent or client.

4.3   Execution-Only

A firm carries out transactions on an execution-only basis if the customer asks it to buy or sell a specific named investment product without having been prompted or advised by the firm. In such instances, customers are responsible for their own decision about a product's suitability.

The practice of execution-only sales is long-established. To ensure that firms operate within regulatory guidelines they need to record and retain evidence in writing that the firm:

* gave no advice; and
* made it clear, at the time of the sale, that it was not responsible for the product's suitability.

END OF CHAPTER QUESTIONS

Think of an answer for each question and refer to the appropriate section for confirmation.

Question	Answer Reference
1. What are the main activities undertaken by the professional financial services sector?	Section 2
2. What is the main service provided by international banks?	Section 2
3. How does a mutual savings institution differ from a retail bank?	Section 3.1
4. What are the main types of services provided by investment banks?	Section 3.3
5. What is protection planning and what scenarios can protection policies provide cover for?	Section 3.5
6. What services does a custodian offer?	Section 3.8
7. What is the role of a third party administrator?	Section 3.10
8. What are the types of financial adviser and how does the range of products they advise on differ?	Section 4.1
9. What is a platform and why are they a useful distribution channel?	Section 4.2
10. What records should be kept where a transaction is undertaken on an execution-only basis?	Section 4.3

CHAPTER TWO

ECONOMIC ENVIRONMENT

This syllabus area will provide approximately 3 of the 50 examination questions

In this next chapter, we turn to the broader economic environment in which the financial services industry operates.

First, we will look at how economic activity is determined in various economic and political systems and then look at the role of the Bank of England in the management of that economic activity.

The chapter concludes with an explanation of some of the key economic measures that provide an indication of the state of an economy.

1.   FACTORS DETERMINING ECONOMIC ACTIVITY

LEARNING OBJECTIVES

2.1.1   Know the factors which determine the level of economic activity:
          state-controlled economies; market economies; mixed economies;
          open economies

1.1   State-Controlled Economies

A state-controlled economy is one in which the state (in the form of the government) decides what is produced and how it is distributed. The best-known example of a state-controlled economy is the Soviet Union throughout most of the 20th century.

Sometimes these economies are referred to as 'planned economies' because the production and allocation of resources is planned in advance, rather than being allowed to respond to market forces. However, the need for careful planning and control can bring about excessive layers of bureaucracy and state control inevitably removes a great deal of individual choice.

These factors have contributed to the reform of the economies of the former Soviet states and the introduction of a more 'mixed' economy (covered in more detail in Section 1.3).

1.2   Market Economies

In a market economy the forces of supply and demand determine how resources are allocated.

Businesses produce goods and services to meet the demand from consumers. The interaction of demand from consumers and supply from businesses in the market will determine the market-clearing price. This is the price that reflects the balance between what consumers will willingly pay for goods and services and what suppliers will willingly accept for them.

If there is oversupply, the price will be low and some producers will leave the market. If there is undersupply, the price will be high, which will attract new producers into the market.

There is not only a market for goods and services, but also for productive assets, such as capital goods, eg, machinery, labour and money. For the labour market, it is the wage level that is effectively the 'price' and for the money market it is the interest rate.

People compete for jobs and companies compete for customers in a market economy. Scarce resources, including skilled labour, such as a football player, or a financial asset, such as a share in a successful company, will have a high value. In a market economy, competition means that inferior football players and shares in unsuccessful companies will be much cheaper and ultimately competition could bring about the collapse of the unsuccessful company or the football player searching for an alternative career.

1.3   Mixed Economies

A mixed economy combines a market economy with some element of state control. The vast majority of economies are mixed to a greater or lesser extent.

While most of us would agree that unsuccessful companies should be allowed to fail, we generally feel that the less able in society should be cushioned from the full force of the market economy.

In a mixed economy, the government will provide a welfare system to support the unemployed, the infirm and the elderly, in tandem with the market-driven aspects of the economy. Governments will also spend money running key areas like defence, education, public transport, health and police services.

Governments finance their public expenditure by:

*   collecting taxes directly from wage earners and companies;
*   collecting indirect taxes (eg, VAT and taxes on petrol, cigarettes and alcohol); and
*   raising money through borrowing in the capital markets.

Civil servants, primarily working for the government to raise money and spend it, tend to be one of the largest groups in the labour market. In the UK it is the civil servants working for the treasury who raise money and allocate it to the 'spending departments', such as the National Health Service.

1.4   Open Economies

In an open economy there are few barriers to trade or controls over foreign exchange.

Although most western governments create barriers to protect their citizens against illegal drugs and other dangers, they generally have policies to allow or encourage free trade.

From time to time, issues will arise where one country believes another is taking unfair advantage of trade policies and will take some form of retaliatory action, possibly including the imposition of sanctions. When a country prevents other countries from trading freely with it in order to preserve its domestic market, it is usually referred to as protectionism.

The World Trade Organisation exists to promote the growth of free trade between economies.

It is, therefore, sometimes called on to arbitrate when disputes arise.

2.   ROLE OF THE BANK OF ENGLAND

LEARNING OBJECTIVES

2.1.2   Know the functions of the Bank of England

2.1.3   Know the functions of the monetary policy committee

BANK OF ENGLAND   The UK's central bank, the Bank of England, was founded in 1694 but it was not until 1997, when the Bank of England's Monetary Policy Committee (MPC) was established, that the Bank gained operational independence in setting UK monetary policy in line with that of most other developed nations.

The process had previously been subject to the possibility of political interference.

The MPC's primary focus is to ensure that inflation is kept within a government-set range. It does this by setting the 'base rate', an officially published short-term interest rate and is the MPC's sole policy instrument.

At its monthly meetings, the MPC must gauge all of those factors that can influence inflation over both the short and medium-term. These include the level of the exchange rate, the rate at which the economy is growing, how much consumers are borrowing and spending, wage inflation and any changes to government spending and taxation plans. When setting the base rate, however, it must also be mindful of the impact any changes will have on the sustainability of economic growth and employment in the UK and the lag between a change in rate and the effects it will have on the economy. Depending on which sector of the economy we are looking at, this can be a very short period of time (eg, credit card spending when consumers are already stretched), to up to 12 months (businesses altering their investment and expansion plans).

In addition to its short-term interest rate-setting role, the Bank also assumes responsibility for all other traditional central bank activities with the exception of supervising the banking system, managing the national debt and providing a depositors' protection scheme for bank deposits.

The other traditional central bank activities that the Bank undertakes include:

*   Acting as banker to the banking system by accepting deposits from, and lending to, commercial banks.
*   Acting as banker to the government.
*   Acting as lender of last resort to the banking system in financial crises to prevent its systemic collapse.
*   Issuing notes and coins.
*   Holding the nation's gold and foreign currency reserves.
*   Influencing the value of a nation's currency through activities such as intervention in the currency markets.

3.   IMPACT OF INFLATION

LEARNING OBJECTIVES

2.1.4   Know how goods and services are paid for and how credit is created

In this section we look at the impact of inflation. We will look firstly at how goods and services are paid for, how credit is created and examine its interaction with inflation.

3.1   Credit Creation

Most of what we buy is not paid for using cash. We find it more convenient to pay by card or cheque.

It is fairly easy (subject to the borrower's credit status) to buy something now and pay later, for example, by going overdrawn, using a credit card or taking out a loan. Loans will often be for more substantial purchases such as a house or a car. Buying now and paying later is generally referred to as purchasing goods and services 'on credit'.

The banking system provides a mechanism in which credit can be created. This means that banks can increase the total amount of money supply in the economy.

EXAMPLE

New Bank plc sets up business and is granted a banking licence. It is authorised to take deposits and make loans. Because New Bank knows that only a small proportion of the deposited funds are likely to be demanded at any one time, it will be able to lend the deposited money to others. New Bank will make profits by lending money out at a higher rate than it pays depositors.

These loans provide an increase in the money supply in circulation – New Bank is creating credit.

By this action of lending to borrowers, banks create money and advance this to industry, consumers and governments. This money circulates within the economy, being spent on goods and services by the people who have borrowed it from the banks. The people to whom it is paid (the providers of those goods and services) will then deposit it in their own bank accounts, allowing the banks to use it to create fresh credit all over again. It is estimated that this 'credit creation' process accounts for 96% of the money in circulation in most industrialised nations, with only 4% being in the form of notes and coins created by the government.

If this process were uncontrolled it would lead to a rapid increase in the money supply and with too much money chasing too few goods, the result would be an increase in inflation.

Understandably, therefore, central banks aim to keep the amount of credit creation under control as part of their overall monetary policy. They will aim to ensure that the amount of credit creation is below the level at which it would increase the money supply so much that inflation accelerates. Nowadays, the UK's central bank (the Bank of England) does this by influencing peoples' appetite for borrowing through the interest rate, as we saw earlier. It no longer has direct responsibility for limiting banks' lending activity as this is overseen by the UK's financial services regulator, the Financial Services Authority (FSA).

3.2   Impact of Inflation

LEARNING OBJECTIVES

2.1.5   Understand the impact of inflation on economic behaviour

Inflation is a persistent increase in the general level of prices. There are a number of reasons for prices to increase, such as excess demand in the economy, scarcity of resources and key workers, or rapidly increasing government spending. Most western governments seek to control inflation at a level of about 2–3% per annum without letting it get too high (or too low).

High levels of inflation can cause problems:

- Businesses have to continually update prices to keep pace with inflation.
- Employees find the real value of their salaries eroded.
- Those on fixed levels of income, like pensioners, will suffer as the price increases are not matched by increases in income.
- Exports may become less competitive.
- The real value of future pensions and investment income becomes difficult to assess, which might act as a disincentive to save.

There are, however, some positive aspects to high levels of inflation:

- Rising house prices contribute to a 'feel good' factor (although this might contribute to further inflation as house owners become more eager to borrow and spend).
- Borrowers benefit, because the value of borrowers' debt falls in 'real terms' – ie, after adjusting for the effect of inflation.

4.   KEY ECONOMIC INDICATORS

LEARNING OBJECTIVES

2.1.6   Know the meaning of the following measures of inflation: retail price
           index; RPIX; consumer price index

As well as being essential to the management of the economy, key economic indicators can provide
investors with a guide to the health of the economy and aid long-term investment decisions. Section 4.1
looks at some of the main indicators.

4.1   Economic Measures

There are various measures of inflation:

*   **Retail Price Index (RPI).** The RPI (also known as the 'headline' rate) measures the increase
    in general household spending, including mortgage and rent payments, food, transport and
    entertainment.
*   **RPIX.** This is the RPI, excluding mortgage interest payments. This is often referred to as the
    'underlying' rate of inflation. Excluding mortgage interest payments removes much of the impact of
    interest rate changes in general from the measure of inflation.
*   **Consumer Price Index (CPI).** This is a measure of inflation that is prepared in a standard way
    throughout the European Union (EU). Like RPIX, it excludes mortgage interest payments, mostly
    because a large proportion of the population in continental Europe rent their homes, rather than
    buy them. Unlike the RPIX, however, it also excludes other housing costs aside from mortgage
    interest costs (for example, it excludes the 'depreciation component', an amount which the RPI
    uses to allow for the cost of maintaining a home in a constant condition).
*   **Harmonised Index of Consumer Prices.** This is the measure of inflation that is prepared in a
    standard way throughout the European Union (EU).

In the UK, the government uses the CPI for a range of purposes, principally those where it needs
to measure inflation on a like-for-like basis with those other European countries that use the same
standard method of calculation.

4.2   Measures of Economic Data

LEARNING OBJECTIVES

2.1.7   Know the impact of the following economic data: gross domestic
           product (GDP), balance of payments, public sector net cash
           requirement (PSNCR), level of unemployment

In addition to inflation measures like the RPI, there are a number of other economic statistics carefully
watched by the government and by other market participants as potentially significant indicators of how
the economy is performing.

4.2.1 Gross Domestic Product (GDP)

GDP is a measure of a country's output. It is calculated quarterly as the total of:

Gross Domestic Product	
	Consumer spending
Plus	Government spending
Plus	Investment
Plus	Exports
Less	Imports
Equals	GDP

A steadily increasing GDP is generally an indication of a healthy economy, while two quarters of successive declining growth are defined as a recession.

HOTSPOT 	Go online to your elearning product for further information on GDP.
2	If you haven't purchased your elearning product, you can order now by calling Client Services on +44(0)20 7645 0680.

4.2.2 Balance of Payments

The balance of payments is a summary of all the transactions between the UK and the rest of the world. If the UK imports more than it exports, there is a balance of payments deficit. If the UK exports more than it imports, there is a balance of payment surplus.

4.2.3 Public Sector Net Cash Requirement (PSNCR)

The PSNCR is the difference between government expenditure and government income, mainly from taxes. In a buoyant economy, government spending tends to be less than income, with substantial tax revenues generated from corporate profits and high levels of employment. This enables the government to reduce public sector (ie, government) borrowing.

In a slowing economy, spending tends to exceed tax revenues and the government will need to raise borrowing by issuing government bonds. This is currently the case in the UK where the budget deficit has exploded over 2009 as the recession has reduced tax receipts and pushed up spending on unemployment benefit. At the time of writing, the national debt had soared to 59.2% of GDP, which is its highest level since records began in 1974/75.

As mentioned earlier, excessive government spending, causing a growing PSNCR, is likely to bring about an increase in the rate of inflation.

4.2.4 Level of Unemployment

The extent to which those seeking employment cannot find work is an important indicator of the health of the economy. There is always likely to be some unemployment in an economy – some people might lack the right skills and/or live in employment black spots. Higher levels of unemployment indicate low demand in the economy for goods and services produced or sold in the UK and therefore, low demand for UK people to provide them.

In addition, high unemployment levels will have a negative impact on the government's finances. The government will need to increase social security payments and income will decrease because of the lack of tax revenues from the unemployed.

END OF CHAPTER QUESTIONS

Think of an answer for each question and refer to the appropriate section for confirmation.

Question	Answer Reference
1. What are the key differences between state-controlled and market economies?	Sections 1.1 & 1.2
2. Which international organisation has the role of reducing trade barriers?	Section 1.4
3. What is the primary role of the Monetary Policy Committee?	Section 2
4. What would be the effect of uncontrolled growth in the money supply?	Section 3.1
5. What are the negative effects of inflation?	Section 3.2
6. What are the principal differences between RPI, RPIX and the CPI?	Section 4.1
7. What economic measure is used as an indicator of the health of the economy?	Section 4.2.1
8. What does the balance of payments represent?	Section 4.2.2
9. What is the potential impact of increasing levels of government spending?	Section 4.2.3
10. What is the impact of high unemployment levels on the economy?	Section 4.2.4

CHAPTER THREE

FINANCIAL ASSETS & MARKETS

This syllabus area will provide approximately 7 of the 50 examination questions

This chapter provides an overview of the main asset classes and looks at the foreign exchange, derivatives and commodities markets and the main world stock markets. Subsequent chapters will look in more detail at equities, bonds and derivatives.

1. CASH DEPOSITS

LEARNING OBJECTIVES

3.1.1   Know the characteristics of fixed term and instant access deposit accounts

3.1.2   Understand the distinction between gross and net interest payments

3.1.3   Be able to calculate the net interest due given the gross interest rate, the deposited sum, the period and tax rate

3.1.4   Know the advantages and disadvantages of investing in cash

Nearly all investors keep at least part of their wealth in the form of cash which will be deposited with a bank or other savings institution to earn interest.

Cash deposits comprise accounts held with banks or other savings institutions, such as building societies. They are held by a wide variety of depositors – from retail investors, through to companies, governments and financial institutions.

The main characteristics of cash deposits are:

• The return simply comprises interest income with no potential for capital growth.
• The amount invested (the 'capital') is repaid in full at the end of the investment term or when withdrawn.

The interest rate paid on deposits will vary with the amount of money deposited. Large deposits are more economical for the bank or building society to process and will earn a better rate. The rate will also vary because of competition as deposit-taking institutions will compete intensely with one another to attract new deposits.

Generally, receipt of interest by an individual is subject to income tax. For most deposits, tax is deducted 'at source' – that is, by the deposit-taker before paying the interest to the depositor. Where this happens, tax is deducted at a flat 20% (regardless of the depositor's tax rate).

The 'headline' rate of interest quoted by deposit-takers, before deduction of tax, is referred to as the **gross interest** and the rate of interest after tax is deducted is referred to as **net interest**.

EXAMPLE

To keep the calculation simple, let us assume Mrs Jones is entitled to 5% gross interest on £200 deposited in **XYZ Bank** for a year.

She will earn **£200 x 5% = £10** interest on her bank deposit before the deduction of any tax.

She will receive net interest of **£8** from **XYZ Bank**.

XYZ Bank will subsequently pay the £2 of tax on behalf of Mrs Jones to HM Revenue & Customs.

This can be summarised as follows:

Gross interest earned: £200 x 5% =	£10
Tax deducted by XYZ Bank and paid to HM Revenue & Customs: 20% x £10	(£2)
Net interest received by Mrs Jones: £10 x 80%	£8

For a basic rate taxpayer, the tax deducted at source means that no further tax is payable. For a higher rate taxpayer, liable to tax at 40%, a further 20% will have to be paid when she submits her tax return.

Non-taxpayers, such as those on very low incomes, can submit a form known as an 'R85'. This enables interest to be paid gross, with no deduction of tax at source. This is much easier than having tax deducted at source and filling out and submitting a tax reclaim form.

At the end of the tax year, depositors receive a tax certificate from the savings institution which confirms that the basic rate of tax has been paid on their behalf.

EXERCISE 1

Mr Evans is a basic rate taxpayer. He has had £3,000 on deposit at XYZ Bank for a year, earning 4% gross interest. How much interest does Mr Evans receive, and how much is deducted at source on his behalf?

EXERCISE 2

Alan is 12 years old and his father has submitted an R85 form on his behalf. Alan has had £400 on deposit at XYZ Bank for a year, earning 3% gross interest. How much interest does Alan receive, and how much is deducted at source on his behalf?

The answers to these exercises can be found at the end of this chapter.

Bank and building society deposits are usually also protected by a compensation scheme. This will repay any deposited money lost, up to a set maximum, as a result of the collapse of a bank or building society. The sum is fixed so as to be of meaningful protection to most retail investors, although it would be of less help to very substantial depositors.

Although cash investments are relatively simple products, it does not follow that they are free of risks as 2008 so clearly demonstrated.

It should also be noted that cash investments are not a designated investment. As a result, they do not fall within the scope of the Financial Services and Markets Act 2000 (FSMA), with the exception of money market funds and cash-based individual savings accounts. Although most cash products are not regulated, the Financial Services Authority does regulate banks and other deposit takers and depositors based in the UK are covered by the Financial Services Compensation Scheme (FSCS). The FSCS provides protection for the first £50,000 of deposits per person with an authorised institution.

Some of the risks presented by cash-based investments include:

- Deposit-taking institutions are of varying creditworthiness; default risk must be assessed.
- Inflation reduces returns and could mean the real return after tax is negative.
- Interest rates change and so the returns from cash deposits will vary.
- Currency risk and different regulatory regimes where funds are invested offshore.

As a result, when comparing available investment options it is important to consider the risks that exist as well as comparing the interest rates available.

2. MONEY MARKETS

LEARNING OBJECTIVES

3.2.1   Know the difference between a capital market instrument and a money market instrument

3.2.2   Know the definition and features of the following: treasury bill; commercial paper; certificate of deposit

3.2.3   Know the advantages and disadvantages of investing in money market instruments

The money markets are the wholesale or institutional markets for cash and are characterised by the issue, trading and redemption of short-dated negotiable securities. These usually have a maturity of up to one year, though three months is more typical.

Due to the short-term nature of the market most instruments are issued in bearer form and at a discount to their face value to save on the administration associated with registration and the payment of interest. (An explanation of 'bearer' can be found in the next chapter.) Although accessible to retail investors indirectly through collective investment funds, direct investment in money market instruments is often subject to a relatively high minimum subscription and, therefore, tends to be more suitable for institutional investors.

Cash deposits and money market instruments provide a low risk way to generate an income or capital return, as appropriate, while preserving the nominal value of the amount invested. They also provide a valuable role in times of market uncertainty. However, they are unsuitable for anything other than the short-term as, historically, they have underperformed most other asset types over the medium- to long-term. Moreover, in the long-term, return from cash deposits, once tax and inflation have been taken into account, has barely been positive.

The main types of UK money market instruments are:

- **Treasury Bills.** These are issued weekly by the Debt Management Office (DMO) on behalf of the treasury. The money is used for the government's short-term borrowing needs. Treasury bills are non-interest bearing instruments (sometimes referred to as 'zero coupon' instruments). Instead of interest being paid out on them, they are issued at a discount to par – ie, a price of less than £100 per £100 nominal (the amount of the treasury bill that will be repaid on maturity) and commonly redeem after three months. For example, a treasury bill might be issued for £990 and mature at £1,000 three months later. The investor's return is the difference between the £990 he paid, and the £1,000 he receives on the treasury bill's maturity.
- **Certificates of Deposit (CDs).** These are issued by banks in return for deposited money: you could think of them as tradable deposit accounts, as they can be bought and sold in the same way that shares are. For example, Lloyds Banking Group might issue a CD to represent a deposit of £1 million from a customer, redeemable in six months. The CD might specify that Lloyds TSB will pay the £1 million back plus interest of, say, 2.5% of £1 million. If the customer needs the money back before six months has elapsed, he can sell the CD to another investor in the money market.
- **Commercial Paper (CP).** This is the corporate equivalent of a treasury bill. Commercial paper is issued by large companies to meet their short-term borrowing needs. A company's ability to issue commercial paper is typically agreed with banks in advance. For example, a company might agree with its bank to a programme of £10 million worth of commercial paper. This would enable the company to issue various forms of commercial paper with different maturities (eg, one month, three months and six months) and possibly different currencies, to the bank. As with treasury bills, commercial paper is zero coupon and issued at a discount to its par value.

Settlement of money market instruments is typically achieved through CREST and is commonly settled on the day of the trade or the following business day.

3. PROPERTY

LEARNING OBJECTIVES

3.3.1 Know the characteristics of the property market:
commercial/residential property; direct/indirect investment

3.3.2 Know the advantages and disadvantages of investing in property

Property as an asset class is unique in its distinguishing features:

- Each individual property is unique in terms of location, structure and design.
- Valuation is subjective as property is not traded in a centralised marketplace and continuous and reliable price data is not available.
- It is subject to complex legal considerations and high transaction costs upon transfer.
- It is highly illiquid as a result of not being instantly tradable.
- It is also illiquid in another sense: the investor generally has to sell all of the property, or nothing at all. It is not generally feasible for a commercial property investor to sell one flat out of an entire block (or, at least, to do so would be commercially unattractive) – and a residential property owner cannot sell his spare bedroom to raise a little cash!
- Since property can only be purchased in discrete and sizeable units, diversification is made difficult.
- The supply of land is finite and its availability can be further restricted by legislation and local planning regulations. Therefore, price is predominantly determined by changes in demand.

What is also fundamentally different is the price. Only the largest investors, which generally means institutional investors, can purchase sufficient properties to build a diversified portfolio. They tend to avoid residential property (although some have diversified into sizeable residential property portfolios) and, instead, they concentrate on commercial property, industrial property and farmland.

Many private investors have chosen to become involved in the property market through the buy-to-let market. Other smaller investors, wanting to include property within a diversified portfolio, instead generally seek indirect exposure via a collective investment scheme, property bonds issued by insurance companies or shares in publicly quoted property companies.

Direct investment in property does, however, confer a number of advantages. As an asset class, it has consistently provided positive real long-term returns, allied to low volatility and a reliable stream of income.

However, property can be subject to prolonged downturns and its lack of liquidity, significant maintenance costs, high transactions costs on transfer and the risk of having commercial property with no tenant (and, therefore, no rental income) really makes commercial property suitable as an investment only for long-term investing institutions such as pension funds.

The availability of indirect investment media, however, makes property a more accessible asset class to those running smaller, diversified portfolios.

4.   FOREIGN EXCHANGE

LEARNING OBJECTIVES

3.4.1   Know the basic structure of the foreign exchange market including spot and forward rates

The foreign exchange market, which is also known as the Forex or FX market, refers to the trading of one currency for another. It is by far the largest market in the world.

Historically, currencies were backed by gold (as money had 'intrinsic value'); this prevented the value of money from being debased and triggering inflation. This gold standard was replaced after the Second World War with the Bretton Woods Agreement. This agreement aimed to prevent speculation in currency markets, by fixing all currencies against the dollar and making the dollar convertible to gold at a fixed rate of $35 per ounce. Under this system, countries were prohibited from devaluing their currencies by more than 10%, which they might have been tempted to do to improve their trade position.

The growth of international trade and increasing pressure for the movement of capital eventually destabilised this agreement, and it was finally abandoned in the 1970s. Currencies were allowed to float freely against one another, leading to the development of new financial instruments and speculation in the currency markets.

Trading in currencies became 24 hour as it could take place in the various time zones of Asia, Europe and America. London, being placed between the Asian and American time zones, was well placed to take advantage of this and has grown to become the world's largest Forex market.

Other large centres include the US, Japan and Singapore.

The Forex market is renowned for being an over-the-counter (OTC) market where brokers and dealers negotiate directly with one another. The main participants are large international banks which continually provide the market with both bid (buy) and ask (sell) prices. Central banks are also major participants in foreign exchange markets, which they use to try to control money supply, inflation and interest rates.

There are several types of transactions and financial instruments commonly used:

- **Spot.** The 'spot rate' is the rate quoted by a bank for the exchange of one currency for another with immediate effect (NB: in many cases, however, spot trades are 'settled' – that is, the currencies actually change hands and arrive in recipients' bank accounts two business days after the transaction date).
- **Forward transaction.** In this type of transaction, money does not actually change hands until some agreed upon future date. A buyer and seller agree on an exchange rate for any date in the future, for a fixed sum of money, and the transaction occurs on that date, regardless of what the market rates are then. The duration of the trade can be a few days, months or years.
- **Futures.** Foreign currency futures are a standardised version of forward transactions that are traded on derivatives exchanges for standard sizes and maturity dates. The average contract length is roughly three months.

- **Swap.** The most common type of forward transaction is the currency swap. In a swap, two parties exchange currencies for a certain length of time and agree to reverse the transaction at a later date. These are not exchange-traded contracts and instead are negotiated individually between the parties to a swap. They are a type of OTC derivative and are covered in the next section.

5. DERIVATIVES & COMMODITY MARKETS

LEARNING OBJECTIVES

3.5.1   Know the characteristics of the derivatives and commodity markets: trading (metals, energy)

3.5.2   Know the advantages and disadvantages of investing in the derivatives and commodity markets

A derivative is a financial instrument whose price is derived from that of another asset (the other asset being known as the 'underlying asset', or sometimes 'underlying' for short).

Derivatives are often thought of as dangerous instruments that are impenetrably complex. Whilst derivatives can be complex and present systemic risks, they are chiefly designed to be used to reduce the risk faced by organisations and individuals, a process known as hedging. Equally, many derivatives are not particularly complex.

As an example, imagine that you wanted to purchase a large amount of wheat from a wholesale supplier. You contact the supplier and see that it will cost £5 a bushel. But you discover that the wheat is currently out of stock in the warehouse. However, you can sign a contract to accept delivery of the wheat in one months' time (when the stock will be replenished) and at that stage the store will charge the £5 for each bushel you order now. If you sign, you have agreed to defer delivery for one month – and you have purchased into a derivative.

The physical trading of commodities takes place side by side with the trading of derivatives. The physical market concerns itself with procuring, transporting and consuming real commodities by the shipload on a global basis. This trade is dominated by major international trading houses, governments plus the major producers and consumers. The derivative markets exist in parallel and serve to provide a price-fixing mechanism whereby all stakeholders in the physical market can hedge market price risk. Another aspect of commodity markets, more recent in origin but highly developed, is the use of commodities as an investment asset class in its own right.

5.1   Physical Markets

There are a number of different commodity markets which are differentiated by the commodity that is traded there. Some of the main ones are:

- agricultural markets;
- base and precious metals;
- energy markets;
- power markets;
- plastics markets;
- emissions markets;
- freight and shipping markets.

We will consider the features of the base and precious metals markets and energy markets below.

5.1.1   Base and Precious Metals

There are numerous metals produced worldwide and, subsequently, refined for use in a large variety of products and processes.

As with all other commodity prices, metal prices are influenced by supply and demand. The factors influencing supply include the availability of raw materials and the costs of extraction and production.

Demand comes from underlying users of the commodity, for example, the growing demand for metals in rapidly industrialising economies, including China and India.

It also originates from investors such as hedge funds who might buy metal futures in anticipation of excess demand or incorporate commodities into specific funds. Producers use the market for hedging their production. Traditionally, the price of precious metals such as gold will rise in times of crisis – gold is seen as a safe haven.

5.1.2   Energy Markets

The energy market includes the market for oil (and other oil-based products like petroleum), natural gas and coal.

Oil includes both crude oil and various 'fractions' produced as a result of the refining process, such as naptha, butanes, kerosene, petrol and heating/gas oil. Crude oil is defined by three primary factors:

- Field of origin, for example, Brent, West Texas Intermediate, Dubai.
- Density, ie, low density or 'light', high density or 'heavy'.
- Sulphur content, ie, low sulphur (known as 'sweet') or high sulphur (known as 'sour').

Supply of these commodities is finite, and countries with surplus oil and gas reserves are able to export to those countries with insufficient oil and gas to meet their requirements. Prices could be raised by producers restricting supply, for example, by the activities of the major oil producers in the Organisation of the Petroleum Exporting Countries (OPEC).

Demand for oil and gas is ultimately driven by levels of consumption, which in turn is driven by energy needs, for example, from manufacturing industry and transport. Prices can react sharply to political crises, particularly in major oil producing regions of the world such as the Middle East.

Furthermore, since the level of demand is directly determined by the consuming economies' growth, economic forecasts and economic data also have an impact on energy prices.

5.2   Derivatives Markets

Broadly speaking, there are two distinct groups of derivatives which are differentiated by how they are traded. They are **OTC derivatives** and **exchange-traded derivatives**.

OTC derivatives are ones that are negotiated and traded privately between parties without the use of an exchange. Products such as interest rate swaps, forward rate agreements and other exotic derivatives are mainly traded in this way.

The OTC market is the larger of the two in terms of value of contracts traded daily. Trading takes place predominantly in Europe and, particularly, in the UK.

Exchange-traded derivatives are ones that have standardised features and can, therefore, be traded on an organised exchange, such as single stock or index derivatives. The main types are futures and options, which are considered later in the workbook. The role of the exchange is to provide a marketplace for trading to take place but also to stand between each party to a trade to provide a guarantee that the trade will eventually be settled. It does this by acting as an intermediary for all trades and by requiring participants to post a margin, which is a proportion of the value of the trade, for all transactions that are entered into.

Details of some of the main derivatives exchanges in Europe are shown below.

5.3   NYSE Liffe

In 2001, Euronext purchased a derivatives exchange in London called LIFFE (pronounced 'life') and renamed it Euronext.liffe. LIFFE was originally an acronym for the London International Financial Futures and Options Exchange, originally set up in 1982. Euronext is a network of individual European stock exchanges formed by the exchanges in Paris, Amsterdam and Brussels. Euronext has since merged with the New York Stock Exchange to become the NYSE Euronext Group and the exchange is now known as NYSE Liffe.

NYSE Liffe is the main exchange for trading financial derivative products in the UK, including futures and options on:

- interest rates and bonds;
- equity indices (eg, FTSE); and
- individual equities (eg, BP, HSBC).

NYSE Liffe also trades derivatives on soft commodities, such as sugar, wheat and cocoa. It also runs futures and options markets in Amsterdam, Brussels, Lisbon and Paris.

Trading on NYSE Liffe is on an electronic, computer-based system, known as Liffe CONNECT.

5.4   Eurex

Eurex is the world's leading international derivatives exchange and is based in Frankfurt. Its principal products are German bond futures and options, the most well known of which are contracts on the Bund (a German bond). It also trades index products for a range of European markets.

Eurex was created by Deutsche Börse AG and the Swiss Exchange. Trading is on the fully computerised Eurex platform and its members are linked to the Eurex system via a dedicated wide-area communications network (WAN). This enables members from across Europe and the US to access Eurex outside Switzerland and Germany.

5.5   IntercontinentalExchange (ICE)

ICE operates the electronic global futures and OTC marketplace for trading energy commodity contracts. These contracts include crude oil and refined products, natural gas, power and emissions.

The company's regulated futures and options business, formerly known as the International Petroleum Exchange (IPE), now operates under the name ICE Futures. ICE acquired the London-based energy futures and options exchange in 2001 and completed the transition from open-outcry to electronic trading in April 2005.

ICE Futures is Europe's leading energy futures and options exchange. ICE's products include derivative contracts based on key energy commodities: crude oil and refined oil products, such as heating oil and jet fuel and other products, like natural gas and electric power.

Recently, ICE Futures introduced what has become Europe's leading emissions futures contract in conjunction with the European Climate Exchange (ECX).

5.6   London Metal Exchange (LME)

The London Metal Exchange is the world's premier non-ferrous metals market and has been operating for over 130 years. Although it is based in London, it is a global market with an international membership and with more than 95% of its business coming from overseas.

Futures and options contracts are traded on a range of metals, including aluminium, copper, nickel, tin, zinc and lead. More recently, it has also launched the world's first futures contracts for plastics.

Trading on the LME takes place across three trading platforms: through open-outcry trading in the 'ring', through an inter-office telephone market and through LME Select, the exchange's electronic trading platform.

6. WORLD STOCK MARKETS

LEARNING OBJECTIVES

3.6.1   Know the characteristics of the following exchanges: London Stock
         Exchange; New York Stock Exchange; NASDAQ; Euronext; Tokyo
         Stock Exchange; Deutsche Börse

Stock exchanges have been around for hundreds of years and now operate throughout the world.

Companies with stocks traded on an exchange are said to be 'listed' and they must meet specific criteria, which vary across exchanges. Most stock exchanges began as physical meeting places, each with a trading 'floor' where traders made deals face-to-face, however the majority are now electronic.

Below is a brief review of some of the world's stock exchanges.

6.1   United States

The New York Stock Exchange (NYSE) and NASDAQ, comprise almost half of the world's total stock exchange activity. As well as trading domestic US stocks, these exchanges are also involved in the trading of shares in major international companies.

6.1.1   New York Stock Exchange – NYSE/Euronext

The New York Stock Exchange (NYSE) is the largest stock exchange in the world, as measured by its domestic market capitalisation and is significantly larger than any other exchange worldwide. Although it trails NASDAQ for the number of companies quoted on it, it is still larger in terms of the value of shares traded.

The NYSE trades in a continuous auction format, that is, member firms act as auctioneers in an open outcry auction market environment in order to bring buyers and sellers together and to manage the actual auction. This makes it unique in world stock markets but, as more than 50% of its order flow is now delivered to the floor electronically, there are proposals to adopt a hybrid structure combining elements of open outcry and electronic markets.

NYSE merged with Euronext in 2007 to create the world's largest and most liquid exchange. Both exchanges, however, continue to operate independently.

6.1.2   NASDAQ

NASDAQ, the National Association of Securities Dealers Automated Quotations, is an electronic stock exchange with 3,200 companies listed on it. It is the third largest stock exchange by market capitalisation and has the second largest trading volume.

There are a variety of companies traded on the exchange, but it is well known for being a high-tech exchange – that is, many of the companies listed on it are telecoms, media or technology companies; it is typically home to many new, high growth and volatile stocks.

Although it is an electronic exchange, trades are still undertaken through market makers who make a book in specific stocks so that when a broker wants to purchase shares, he does so directly from the market maker.

6.2   Europe

Europe accounts for a number of the top world exchanges, as measured by domestic market capitalisation, with Deutsche Börse, Euronext and the London Stock Exchange being the largest.

6.2.1   London Stock Exchange (LSE)

The London Stock Exchange is the most important exchange in Europe and one of the largest in the world. It has over 3,000 companies listed on it and is the most international of all exchanges, with 350 of the companies coming from 50 different countries.

Its main trading system is SETS (Stock Exchange Trading Service) an automated trading system that operates on an order-driven basis. This means that when a buy and sell price match, an order is automatically executed.

For securities that trade less regularly, the LSE uses the SETSqx (Stock Exchange Trading Service quotes and crosses) and SEAQ (Stock Exchange Automated Quote) systems, where market makers keep the shares liquid. These market makers are required to hold shares of a specific company and set the bid and ask prices, ensuring that there is always a market for the stock.

6.2.2   Euronext

As mentioned above, the New York Stock Exchange (NYSE) and Euronext merged in 2007, although both continue to operate independently.

Euronext is a cross-border exchange that operates equity, bond and derivative markets in Belgium, France, the UK (derivatives only), the Netherlands and Portugal.

Euronext provides listing and trading facilities for a range of instruments including equities and bonds and for investment products such as trackers and investment funds. It is an order-driven market and cash instruments are traded via a harmonised order book.

Euronext is also the majority shareholder in MTS, the electronic exchange that dominates trading in the European government bond market. The MTS market model uses a common trading platform, while corporate governance and market supervision are based on the respective national regulatory regimes.

6.2.3   Deutsche Börse

Deutsche Börse is the main German exchange and provides services that include securities and derivatives trading, transaction settlement, the provision of market information, as well as the development and operation of electronic trading systems.

The cash market comprises both floor trading and a fully electronic trading system. Both platforms provide efficient trading and optimum liquidity.

Xetra is Deutsche Börse's electronic trading system for the cash market and matches buy and sell orders from licensed traders in a central, fully electronic order book.

Floor trading takes place in Frankfurt. Each security is supported by a lead broker who fixes bid and ask prices and either executes incoming orders or manages them in an order book until they are executed or deleted or expire. Less liquid securities can thus also be traded efficiently on the trading floor.

Deutsche Börse also owns the international central securities depositary, Clearstream, which provides integrated banking, custody and settlement services for the trading of fixed-interest securities and shares.

6.3 ASIA

6.3.1 Tokyo Stock Exchange (TSE)

The Tokyo Stock Exchange (TSE) is one of five exchanges in Japan, but is undoubtedly, one of the more important world exchanges.

The TSE uses an electronic, continuous auction system of trading. This means that brokers place orders online and when a buy and sell price match, the trade is automatically executed. Deals are made directly between buyer and seller, rather than through a market maker. The TSE uses price controls so that the price of a stock cannot rise above or fall below a certain point throughout the day. These controls are used to prevent dramatic swings in prices that may lead to market uncertainty or stock crashes. If a major swing in price occurs, the exchange can stop trading on that stock for a specified period of time.

7. STOCK MARKET INDICES

LEARNING OBJECTIVES

3.6.2   Know the types and uses of a stock exchange index

7.1 Stock Indices

Markets worldwide compute one or more index of prices of the shares of their country's large companies. These indices provide a snapshot of how share prices are progressing across the whole group of constituent companies. They also provide a benchmark for investors, allowing them to assess whether their portfolios of shares are outperforming or underperforming the market in general.

Additionally, in recent decades, many indices have provided the basis for derivatives contracts, such as Footsie Futures and Footsie Options. Indices also provide the basis for many tracker products.

Generally, the constituents of these indices are the largest companies, ranked by their market value or market capitalisation (market cap). However, there are also indices which track all constituents of a market, or which focus specifically on the smaller companies listed on that market.

7.2   UK Indices

LEARNING OBJECTIVES

3.6.3   Know the differences between the following London Stock Exchange
         indices: FTSE 100; FTSE 250; FTSE 350; FTSE All Share

In the UK, the indices are provided by FTSE International, originally a joint venture between the *Financial Times* and the stock exchange. The relevant indices in the UK are:

- **FTSE 100** – this is an index of the largest 100 UK companies, commonly referred to as the 'Footsie'. The Footsie covers about 70% of the UK market by value.
- **FTSE 250** – an index of the next 250 medium- or middle-sized (mid cap) companies below the 100.
- **FTSE 350** – a combination of the 100 and the 250 indices. The 350 is broken down into industry sectors, for example, retailing and transport.
- **FTSE All Share** – this index covers over 800 companies (including the FTSE 350) and accounts for about 98% of the UK market by value. It is often used as the benchmark against which diversified share portfolios are assessed.

Reviews of the 100, 250 (and, therefore, the 350) are carried out every three months. Companies whose share price has grown strongly, and whose market capitalisation has increased significantly, will replace those whose price and, hence, market capitalisation is static or falling. The All Share is reviewed annually.

7.3   World Indices

LEARNING OBJECTIVES

3.6.4   Know to which markets the following indices relate: Dow Jones
         Industrial Average, S&P 500, Nikkei 225 CAC40, XETRA Dax, NASDAQ
         Composite

Some of the other main indices that are regularly quoted in the financial press are as follows:

Country	Name	Number of stocks
US	DJIA: (Dow Jones Industrial Average): providing a narrow view of the US stock market	30
US	S&P 500 (Standard & Poor's): providing a wider view of the US stock market	500
US	NASDAQ Composite: focusing on the shares traded on NASDAQ, including many technology companies	3,000+
Japan	NIKKEI 225	225
France	CAC 40	40
Germany	XETRA DAX	30

HOTSPOT

3

Go online to your elearning product for further information on world indices.

If you haven't purchased your elearning product, you can order now by calling Client Services on +44(0)20 7645 0680.

ANSWERS FROM PAGE 24

Exercise 1

Interest earned = £3,000 x 4% = £120

Deducted at source = 20% x £120 = £24

Received by Mr Evans = 80% x £120 = £96

Exercise 2

Interest earned and received by Alan = £400 x 3% = £12

No tax is deducted at source since an R85 form has been submitted.

END OF CHAPTER QUESTIONS

Think of an answer for each question and refer to the appropriate section for confirmation.

Question	Answer Reference
1. How much net interest will be paid on a cash deposit of £10,000 deposited for six months at 2.5% pa, if the tax rate is 20%?	Section 1
2. How is the return on a treasury bill paid?	Section 2
3. What are the advantages and disadvantages of investing in property?	Section 3
4. When will a spot Forex trade settle?	Section 4
5. What are the main types of contract traded on NYSE Liffe and Eurex?	Sections 5.1 & 5.2
6. Emission contracts are traded on which exchange?	Section 5.3
7. Which world stock market operates on an open outcry basis?	Section 6.1.1
8. What is the name of the trading system used in Germany?	Section 6.2.3
9. What is the function of a stock market index?	Section 7.1
10. The CAC40 index relates to which market?	Section 7.3

CHAPTER FOUR

EQUITIES

This syllabus area will provide approximately 6 of the 50 examination questions

1. INTRODUCTION

In this chapter we will look in detail at many of the features of equities and how they are traded.

The chapter starts with how a company is formed, before moving on to the requirements for listing on a stock exchange. We will then consider the features of equities, the benefits and risks of owning shares and how they are traded and settled.

2. COMPANY FORMATION AND ADMINISTRATION

LEARNING OBJECTIVES

4.1.1   Know how a company is formed and the differences between private and public companies

2.1   Forming a Company

Many businesses, large and small, are set up as companies.

To form a simple company is inexpensive and requires the founders of the company to complete a series of documents and lodge these with the appropriate authority. In the UK these documents are required to be lodged with the Registrar of Companies at Companies House.

To form a company, two constitutional documents are required:

*   Memorandum of Association; and
*   Articles of Association.

The **Memorandum of Association** is a document that gives details of the company to the external world. It simply states the name of the company, the location of its registered office, its authorised share capital, its business objectives and whether it is a private or public (plc) company.

The **Articles of Association** detail the relationship between the company and one of its key sources of finance; in other words, its owners. The articles include details such as shareholder rights, the frequency of company meetings and the company's borrowing powers.

2.2   Private and Public Companies

Companies are established either as:

*   Private companies, such as ABC ltd, where ltd stands for limited. Such companies can have just one shareholder.

Or

*   Public companies, such as XYZ plc, where plc stands for public limited company. Plcs have to have a minimum of two shareholders.

It is only plcs that are able to issue shares to the public. As a result, all listed companies are plcs, but not all plcs are listed. It is perfectly possible for a company to 'just be' a plc, and not be listed on a stock exchange.

EXAMPLE

The global bank HSBC Holdings is a public limited company and is listed on a number of worldwide stock exchanges including: the London Stock Exchange, the New York Stock Exchange, the Tokyo Stock Exchange and the Hong Kong Stock Exchange.

By contrast, Virgin Holdings, the business empire of Richard Branson, is a public limited company but is not listed.

'Limited' whether as in 'ltd' or 'plc' means that the liability of shareholders for the debts of the company is limited to the amount they agreed to pay to the company on initial subscription.

EXAMPLE

A UK company is created with a share capital of £100 which is made up of 100 ordinary £1 shares.

Assuming that each share is fully paid, an initial shareholder who subscribes for 20 shares will pay £20.

In the event that the company goes into liquidation, the liability of that shareholder for the company's debts is limited to the amount they subscribed, that is £20.

The position would be different if the shares were only partly paid. For example, the shares might be ordinary £1 shares but only require 50p per share to be paid at the outset, the remainder being payable at some future date. In the event of liquidation, the shareholder may be called on to subscribe the balance to meet the company's debts.

2.3   Company Meetings

LEARNING OBJECTIVES

4.1.6   Know the purpose and format of annual general meetings

Companies must hold Annual General Meetings (AGMs) at which the shareholders are given the opportunity to question the directors about the company's strategy and operations.

The shareholders are also given the opportunity to vote on matters such as the appointment and removal of directors and the payment of the final dividend recommended by the directors.

Most matters put to the shareholders are 'ordinary resolutions', requiring a simple majority of those shareholders voting to be passed.

Matters of major importance, such as a proposed change to the company's constitution, require a 'special resolution' and at least 75% to vote in favour.

Shareholders can either vote in person, or have their vote registered at the meeting by completing a proxy voting form, enabling someone else to register their vote on their behalf.

3.   LISTING

4.1.7   Know the difference between the primary market and secondary market

When a company decides to seek a listing for its shares, the process is known by one of a number of terms:

- becoming 'listed' or 'quoted';
- floating on the stock market;
- 'going public'; or
- making an 'Initial Public Offer' (IPO).

Other relevant terminology is 'primary market' and 'secondary market'. The term primary market refers to the marketing of new shares in a company to investors for the first time. Once they have acquired shares, an investor will at some point wish to dispose of some or all of their shares and will generally do this through a stock exchange. This latter process is referred to as 'dealing on the secondary market'.

Typically, a company making an IPO will have been in existence for many years, and will have grown to a point where it wishes to expand further.

3.1   Advantages and Disadvantages of Listing

4.1.9   Know the advantages and disadvantages of a company obtaining a listing of its shares on the London Stock Exchange

The advantages and disadvantages to be considered carefully include the following:

Advantages:

- **Capital** – an IPO provides the possibility of raising capital and, once listed, further offers of shares are much easier to make.
- If the shares being offered to the public are those of the company's original founders, then the IPO offers them an exit route and a means to convert their holdings into cash.
- **Takeovers** – a listed company could use its shares as payment to acquire the shares of other companies as part of a takeover or merger.
- **Status** – being a listed company should help the business in marketing itself to customers, suppliers and potential employees.

- **Employees** – stock options to key staff are a way of providing incentives and retaining employees, and options to buy listed company shares that are easily sold in the market are even more attractive.

Disadvantages:

- **Regulations** – listed companies must govern themselves in a more open way than private ones and provide detailed and timely information on their financial situation and progress.
- **Takeovers** – listed companies are at risk of being taken over themselves.
- **Short-termism** – shareholders of listed companies tend to exert pressure on the company to reach short-term goals, rather than be more patient and look for longer-term investment and growth.

3.2   Requirements for Listing

LEARNING OBJECTIVES

4.1.8   Know the main requirements for listing on the London Stock Exchange

In the UK, the responsibility for allowing a company to be listed on the LSE rests with a division of the UK regulator, the Financial Services Authority. The division is known as the United Kingdom Listing Authority (UKLA).

A listing on the London Stock Exchange is often referred to as a 'full listing'. This distinguishes it from cases where companies are dealt in on the Alternative Investment Market (AIM), where the requirements are less onerous.

The UKLA has a number of requirements for companies seeking a listing for their shares. These are mainly aimed at making sure the company is sufficiently large and complies with rules on issues, like disclosure of important information, for its shares to be held by members of the public.

The main requirements are:

- The company must be a public limited company (plc).
- The company's expected market capitalisation (the share price multiplied by the number of shares in issue) must be at least £700,000.
- The company should have been trading for at least three years and at least 75% of its business must be supported by a historic revenue, earning record for that period.
- At least 25% of the company's shares should be in public hands or available for purchase by the public. The term 'public' excludes directors of the company and their associates and significant shareholders who hold 5% or more of the company's shares.
- A trading company must demonstrate that it has sufficient working capital for the next 12 months.

Once listed, companies are expected to fulfil rules known as the 'continuing obligations'. For example, they are obliged to issue a half-yearly report and to notify the market of any new, price-sensitive information.

3.3   Alternative Investment Market (AIM)

LEARNING OBJECTIVES

4.1.10   Know the role of the Alternative Investment Market (AIM)

Becoming a fully listed company is not open to any company. Listed status is rightly reserved for large, established companies. Smaller businesses have a range of alternative sources of finance for expansion, including the private equity/venture capital industry and the AIM market.

AIM was established by the LSE as a junior market for younger, smaller companies. Such companies apply to the LSE to join AIM, whereas full listing requires application to the UKLA.

The requirements for a listing on AIM, in comparison to the requirements for a full listing, are as follows:

*   No trading history required, the company could be newly established (three years is needed for a full listing).
*   No minimum market capitalisation required (£700,000 is the minimum for a fully listed company).
*   No requirement for a minimum proportion of the shares to be held by the 'public' (at least 25% of the shares in a fully listed company must be held by outside investors).

A company wanting to gain admission to AIM is required to appoint a nominated adviser (NOMAD) and a nominated broker. The role of the NOMAD is to advise the directors of their responsibilities in complying with AIM rules and the content of the prospectus that accompanies the company's application for admission to AIM. The role of the nominated broker is to make a market and facilitate trading in the company's shares, as well as provide ongoing information about the company to interested parties.

Certain rules are common to both AIM and fully listed companies. They must both release price-sensitive information promptly and produce financial information at the half-yearly (interim) and full year (final) stage.

HOTSPOT **4**	Go online to your elearning product for further information on Alternative Investment markets (AIM).
	If you haven't purchased your elearning product, you can order now by calling Client Services on +44(0)20 7645 0680.

4.   TYPES OF EQUITIES

4.1.2   Know the features and benefits of ordinary and preference shares:
dividend; capital gain; share benefits; right to subscribe for new shares;
right to vote

4.1   Ordinary Shares

The share capital of a company may be made up of ordinary shares and the owners of the ordinary shares own the company. If an individual were fortunate enough to own 20% of Vodafone's ordinary shares, he would own one fifth of Vodafone.

Ordinary shares carry the full risk and reward of investing in a company. If a company does well, its ordinary shareholders will do well.

As the ultimate owners of the company, it is the ordinary shareholders who vote 'yes' or 'no' to each resolution put forward by the company directors at company meetings. For example, an offer to take over a company may be made and the directors may propose that it is accepted but this will have to be subject to a vote by shareholders. If the shareholders vote 'no' then the directors have to think again.

Ordinary shareholders share in the profits of the company by receiving annual (and sometimes more frequent), dividends declared by the company. For example, the company directors will propose a dividend which will need to be ratified by the ordinary shareholders before it is formally declared as payable. The amount of dividend paid will depend on how well the company is doing. However, some companies pay large dividends and others none as they plough all profits made back into the future growth.

If the company does badly, it is the ordinary shareholders that will suffer. If the company closes down, often described as the company being 'wound up', the ordinary shareholders are paid after everybody else.

If there is nothing left, then the ordinary shareholders get nothing. If there is money left after all creditors and preference shareholders have been paid, it all belongs to the ordinary shareholders.

4.2   Preference Shares

Some companies have preference shares as well as ordinary shares. The company's internal rules (their 'Articles of Association') set out how the preference shares differ from the ordinary shares.

Normally, preference shares:

* are non-voting, except in certain special circumstances, such as when their dividends have not been paid;
* pay a fixed dividend each year, the amount being set when they are first issued;
* rank ahead of ordinary shares in terms of being paid back if the company is wound up, up to a limited amount to be repaid.

Preference shares may be non-cumulative, cumulative and/or participating.

If dividends cannot be paid in a particular year, perhaps because the company has insufficient profits, preference shares would get no dividend. However, if they were cumulative preference shares then the dividend entitlement accumulates. Assuming sufficient profits, the cumulative preference shares will have the arrears of dividend paid in the subsequent year. If the shares were non-cumulative the dividend from the first year would be lost.

Participating preference shares entitle the holder to a basic dividend of, say, 3p a year, but the directors can award a bigger dividend in a year where the profits exceed a certain level. In other words, the preference shareholder can participate in bumper profits.

5. BENEFITS OF OWNING SHARES

LEARNING OBJECTIVES

4.1.2   Know the features and benefits of ordinary and preference shares: dividend; capital gain; share benefits; right to subscribe for new shares; right to vote

As we have seen earlier, shares carry risks. As a reward for holding them, shareholders hope to benefit from the success of the company. This reward or return can take one of the following forms.

5.1   Dividends

A dividend is the return that an investor gets for providing the risk capital for a business.

Companies pay dividends out of their profits, which form part of their 'distributable reserves'. Distributable reserves are the post-tax profits made over the life of a company, in excess of dividends paid.

EXAMPLE

Harris plc was formed some years ago. Over the company's life it has made £20 million in profits and paid dividends of £13 million. Distributable reserves at the beginning of the year are, therefore, £7 million.

This year Harris plc makes post-tax profits of £3 million and decides to pay a dividend of £1 million.

At the end of the year distributable reserves are:

	£m
Opening balance	7
Profit after tax for year	3
	10
Dividend	(1)
Closing balance	9

Note, despite only making £3 million in the current year, it would be perfectly legal for Harris plc to pay dividends of more than £3 million, because it can use the undistributed profits from previous years.

This would be described as a 'naked' or 'uncovered' dividend, because the current year's profits were insufficient to fully cover the dividend. Companies occasionally do this, but it is obviously not possible to maintain this long-term.

UK companies seek, where possible, to pay steadily growing dividends. A fall in dividend payments can lead to a negative reaction amongst shareholders and a general fall in the willingness to hold the company's shares, or to provide additional capital.

Potential shareholders will compare the dividend paid on a company's shares with alternative investments. These would include other shares, bonds and bank deposits. This involves calculating the dividend yield.

Some companies have a higher than average dividend yield, which may be for one of the following reasons:

• The company is mature and continues to generate healthy levels of cash, but has limited growth potential, perhaps because the government regulates its selling prices, and so there is no great investor appetite for its shares. Examples are utilities such as water or electricity companies.
• The company has a low share price for some other reason, perhaps because it is, or is expected to be, relatively unsuccessful; its comparatively high current dividend is, therefore, not expected to be sustained and its share price is not expected to rise.

In contrast, some companies might have dividend yields that are relatively low. This is generally because:

- the share price is high, because the company is viewed by investors as having high growth prospects; or
- a large proportion of the profit being generated by the company is being ploughed back into the business, rather than being paid out as dividends.

5.2   Capital Gains

Capital gains can be made on shares if their prices increase over time.

If an investor purchased a share for £3.00, and two years later that share price had risen to £5.00, then the investor has made a £2.00 capital gain. If he does not sell the share, then the gain is described as being 'unrealised'; and he runs the risk of the share price falling before he does realise the shares and 'bank' his profits.

In the recent past, the long-term total financial return from UK equities has been fairly evenly split between dividends and capital gain. Whereas dividends need to be reinvested in order to accumulate wealth, capital gains simply build up. However, the shares need to be sold to realise any capital gains.

5.3   Shareholder Benefits

Some companies provide perks to shareholders, such as a telecoms company offering its shareholders a discounted price on their mobile phones or a shipping company offering cheap ferry tickets. Such trade benefits can be a pleasant bonus for small investors, but are not normally a major factor in investment decisions.

5.4   Right to Subscribe for New Shares

Rights issues are one method by which a company can raise additional capital, with existing shareholders having the right to subscribe for new shares. Rights issues are covered in more detail later in this chapter.

If a company was able to issue new shares to anyone, then existing shareholders could lose control of the company, or at least see their share of ownership diluted. As a result, under UK legislation, existing shareholders in UK companies are given 'pre-emptive' rights to subscribe for new shares. What this means is that they are given the option to subscribe for the new share offering, before it is offered to the wider public, and, in many cases, they receive some compensation if they decide not to do so.

5.5   Right to Vote

Ordinary shareholders have the right to vote on matters presented to them at company meetings. This would include the right to vote on proposed dividends and other matters, such as the appointment, or reappointment, of directors.

The votes are normally allocated on the basis of one share = one vote. The votes are cast in one of two ways:

- The individual shareholder can attend the company meeting and vote.
- The individual shareholder can appoint someone else to vote on his behalf – this is commonly referred to as 'voting by proxy'.

6. RISKS OF OWNING SHARES

LEARNING OBJECTIVES

4.1.3   Understand the risks associated with owning shares: price risk; liquidity risk; issuer risk

Shares are relatively high-risk but have the potential for relatively high returns when a company is successful.

The main risks associated with holding shares can be classified under the following three headings.

6.1   Price Risk

Price risk is the risk that share prices in general might fall. Even though the company involved might maintain dividend payments, investors could face a loss of capital.

For example, worldwide equities fell by nearly 20% in a single day, with some shares falling by even more than this. That day was 19 October 1987, and is known as Black Monday. The Dow Jones index fell by 22.3% on that day, wiping US$500 billion off share prices.

Markets in every country around the world followed suit and collapsed in the same fashion. Central banks intervened to prevent a depression and a banking crisis and, remarkably, the markets recovered much of their losses quite quickly from the worst-ever, one-day crash.

After the 1987 crash, global markets resumed the bull market trend driven by computer technology. The arrival of the internet age sparked suggestions that a new economy was in development and led to a surge in internet stocks.

Many of these stocks were quoted on the NASDAQ exchange which went from 600 to 5,000 by 2000. This led the Chairman of the Federal Reserve to describe investor behaviour as 'irrational exuberance'.

By early 2000, reality started to settle in and the 'dot.com' bubble was firmly popped with NASDAQ crashing to 2,000. Economies went into recession and heralded the decline in world stock markets, which continued in many of them until 2003.

The markets then had a period of growth until the sub-prime crisis and credit crunch brought about another fall in stock markets. In 2008, the NASDAQ composite had its worst-ever fall, declining by 40.54% over the year, the Dow Jones Industrial Average fell 33.84% and the FTSE 100 tumbled 31% in the largest annual drop seen since its launch in 1984.

As well as general collapses in prices, any single company can experience dramatic falls in its share price when it discloses bad news, like the loss of a major contract.

Price risk varies between companies: volatile shares tend to exhibit more price risk than more 'defensive' shares, such as utility companies and general retailers.

6.2   Liquidity Risk

Liquidity risk is the risk that shares may be difficult to sell at a reasonable price or traded quickly enough in the market to prevent a loss. It essentially occurs when there is difficulty in finding a counterparty who is willing to trade in a share.

This typically occurs in respect of shares in 'thinly traded' companies – private companies, or those in which there is not much trading activity.

It can also happen, to a lesser degree, if share prices in general are falling, in which case the spread between the bid price (the price at which dealers will buy shares) and the offer price (the price at which dealers will sell shares) may widen.

EXAMPLE

Prices for ABC plc shares might be 720–722p on a normal day.

To begin to see a capital gain, an investor who buys shares (at 722p) needs the price to rise so that the bid (the price at which he could sell) has risen by more than 2p (eg, from 720 to 723p).

If there was a general market downturn, the dealer might widen the price spread to, say, 700–720 to deter sellers. An investor wanting to sell would be forced to accept the much lower price.

Shares in smaller companies tend to have a greater liquidity risk than shares in larger companies – smaller companies also tend to have a wider price spread than larger, more actively traded, companies.

6.3   Issuer Risk

This is the risk that the issuing company collapses and the ordinary shares become worthless.

In general, it is very unlikely that larger, well-established companies would collapse and the risk could be seen, therefore, as insignificant. However, events such as the collapse of Northern Rock, HBOS, Bradford & Bingley and Woolworths show that the risk is a real and present one and cannot be ignored.

In contrast, shares in new companies, that have not yet managed to report profits, may have a substantial issuer risk.

7.   CORPORATE ACTIONS

LEARNING OBJECTIVES

4.1.4   Know the definition of a corporate action and the difference between mandatory, voluntary and mandatory with options

4.1.5   Understand the following terms: bonus/scrip/capitalisation issues; rights issues; dividend payments; takeover/merger

A corporate action occurs when a company does something that affects its shareholders or bondholders. For example, most companies pay dividends to their shareholders twice a year.

Corporate actions can be classified into three types:

- mandatory;
- mandatory with options;
- voluntary.

A **mandatory corporate action** is one mandated by the company, not requiring any intervention from the shareholders or bondholders themselves. The most obvious example of a mandatory corporate action is the payment of a dividend, since all shareholders automatically receive the dividend.

A **mandatory corporate action with options** is an action that has some sort of default option that will occur if the shareholder does not intervene. However, until the date at which the default option occurs, the individual shareholders are given the choice to go for another option. An example of a mandatory with options corporate action is a rights issue (detailed in Section 7.1).

A **voluntary corporate action** is an action that requires the shareholder to make a decision. An example is a takeover bid – if the company is being bid for, each individual shareholder will need to choose whether to accept the offer.

7.1   Rights Issues

A company may wish to raise additional finance by issuing shares. This might be to provide funds for expansion, or to repay bank loans or bond finance. In such circumstances, it is common for a company to approach its existing shareholders with a 'cash call' – they have already bought some shares in the company, so would they like to buy some more?

UK company law gives a series of protections to existing shareholders. They have pre-emptive rights – the right to buy shares so that their proportionate holding is not diluted. A rights issue can be defined as an offer of new shares to existing shareholders, pro-rata to their initial holdings. Since it is an offer and the shareholders have a choice, rights issues are examples of a mandatory with options type of corporate action.

As an example of a rights issue, the company might offer shareholders the right that for every four shares owned, they can buy one more at a specified price that is at a discount to the current market price.

The initial response to the announcement of a planned rights issue will reflect the market's view of the scheme. If it is to finance expansion, and the strategy makes sense to the investors, the share price could well rise. If the money is to be used to pay large bonuses to mediocre directors, the response might be the opposite.

The company and their investment banking advisers will have to consider the numbers carefully. If the price at which new shares are offered is too high, the cash call might flop. This would be embarrassing – and potentially costly for any institution that has underwritten the issue.

Underwriters of a share issue agree, for a fee, to buy any portion of the issue not taken up in the market at the issue price. The underwriters then sell the shares they have bought when market conditions seem opportune to them, and may make a gain or a loss on this sale.

The underwriters agree to buy the shares if no one else will, and the investment bank will probably underwrite some of the issue itself.

If investors have a very negative view of why a rights issue is being made and what it says for the future of the company, the share price can fall substantially. This was seen with HBOS and RBS where the shares fell below the discounted rights issue price. The rights issues were flops and the underwriters ended up having to take up the new shares.

EXAMPLE

ABC plc has 100 million shares in issue, currently trading at £4.00 each.

To raise finance for expansion, it decides to offer its existing shareholders the right to buy one new share for every five previously held. This would be described as a 1 for 5 rights issue.

The price of the rights would be set at a discount to the prevailing market price, at say £3.50.

Each shareholder is given choices as to how to proceed following a rights issue. For an individual holding five shares in ABC plc, he could:

- Take up the rights, by paying the £3.50 and increasing his holding in ABC plc to six shares.
- Sell the rights on to another investor. The rights entitlement is transferable (often described as 'renounceable') and will have a value because it enables the purchase of a share at the discounted price of £3.50.
- Do nothing. If the investor chooses this option, the company's advisers will sell the rights at the best available price and pass on the proceeds (after charges) to the shareholder.

Alternatively, the investor could sell sufficient of the rights to raise cash and use this to take up the rest.

The share price of the investor's existing shares will also adjust to reflect the additional shares that are being issued. So, in the example above, the investor originally had five shares priced at £4 each, worth £20, and can acquire one new share at £3.50. On taking the rights up, the investor will have six shares worth £23.50 or £3.91 each. The share price will therefore change to reflect the effect of the rights issue once the shares go ex-rights.

The adjusted share price of £3.91 is known as the 'theoretical ex-rights price' – it is theoretical as the actual price will be determined by demand and supply.

The rights can be sold and the price is known as the premium. In the example above, if the theoretical ex-rights price is £3.91 and a new share can be acquired for £3.50, then the right to do so has a value. That value is the premium and would be 41p, although again the actual price would depend upon demand and supply.

7.2 Bonus Issues

A bonus issue (also known as a 'scrip' or 'capitalisation' issue) is a corporate action where the company gives existing shareholders extra shares without them having to subscribe any further funds.

The company is simply increasing the number of shares held by each shareholder and capitalises earnings by transfer to shareholders' funds. It is a mandatory corporate action.

EXAMPLE

ABC plc has 100 million shares in issue, currently trading at £4.00 each.

To raise finance for expansion, it decides to offer its existing shareholders the right to buy one new share for every five previously held. This would be described as a 1 for 5 rights issue.

The price of the rights would be set at a discount to the prevailing market price, at say £3.50.

The reason for making a bonus issue is to increase the liquidity of the company's shares in the market and to bring about a lower share price. If a company's share price becomes too high it may become unattractive to investors.

Traditionally, most large UK companies have tried to keep their share prices below £10. For example, several years ago HSBC shares were trading at about £21 and were subject to a 2:1 scrip issue (two new shares for every one previously held), and the share price fell to £7.

7.3 Dividends

Dividends are an example of a mandatory corporate action and represent the part of a company's profit that is passed to its shareholders.

Dividends for most large UK companies are paid twice a year, with the first dividend being declared by the directors and paid approximately halfway through the year (commonly referred to as the 'interim dividend'). The second dividend is paid after approval by shareholders at the company's AGM, held after the end of the company's financial year and is referred to as the 'final dividend' for the year.

The amount paid per share may vary, as it depends on the overall profitability of the company and any plans it might have for future expansion.

The individual shareholders will receive the dividends either by cheque, or by the money being transferred straight into their bank accounts.

A practical difficulty, especially in a large company, where shares change hands frequently, is determining who the correct person to receive dividends is. The LSE, therefore, has procedures to minimise the extent that people receive dividends they are not entitled to, or fail to receive the dividend to which they are entitled.

The shares are bought and sold with the right to receive the next declared dividend up to the date shortly before the dividend payment is made. Up to that point the shares are described as 'cum-dividend'. If the shares are purchased cum-dividend, the purchaser will receive the declared dividend. At a certain point, between the declaration date and the dividend payment date, the shares go 'ex-dividend'. Buyers of shares when they are ex-dividend are not entitled to the declared dividend.

EXAMPLE

The sequence of events might be as follows:

Holding plc calculates its interim profits (for the six months to 30 June) and decides to pay a dividend of 8p. It announces ('declares') the dividend on 17 August and states that it will be paid to those shareholders who are entered on the shareholders' register on Friday 9 October.

This latter date (always on a Friday) is variously known as the:

- record date;
- register date; or
- books closed date.

Given the record date of Friday 9 October, the LSE sets the ex-dividend date as Wednesday 7 October.

The ex-dividend date is invariably a Wednesday and on this day, the shares will go ex-dividend and should fall in price by 8p. This is because new buyers of Holding plc's shares will not be entitled to the dividend.

Mistakes can happen. If an investor bought shares in Holding plc on 5 October and did not receive the 8p per share dividend, he would ask his broker to claim it on his behalf. The buyer's broker would then recover the money via the seller's broker.

7.4 Takeovers and Mergers

Companies seeking to expand can grow organically by buying other companies. In a takeover, which may be friendly or hostile, one company (the predator) seeks to acquire another company (the target).

In a successful takeover the predator company will buy more than 50% of the shares of the target company. When the predator holds more than half of the shares of the target company, the predator is described as having 'gained control' of the target company. Usually, the predator company will look to buy all of the shares in the target company, perhaps for cash, but usually for shares, or a mixture of cash and shares.

A merger is a similar transaction where the two companies are of similar size and agree to merge their interests. However, in a merger it is usual for one company to exchange new shares for the shares of the other. As a result, the two companies effectively merge together to form a bigger entity.

8. TRADING

LEARNING OBJECTIVES

4.1.11   Know how shares are traded on the London Stock Exchange –
SETS/SEAQ/SETSqx

The LSE has been operating for over 300 years and, throughout its history, its trading methods have evolved.

Twenty years ago trading was face-to-face on the trading floor of the exchange (an open-outcry market). In 1986, the LSE moved to screen-based trading with market makers (firms which undertake to quote both buying and selling prices, continuously, for the companies in which they are market makers) quoting prices and handling telephone responses from interested buyers/sellers. Nowadays, market makers are still used for less liquid stocks, with larger companies' shares traded on an electronic order-based system that automatically matches buyers and sellers.

The London Stock Exchange has undertaken major development of its trading platforms in response to the introduction of the Markets in Financial Instruments Directive (MiFID). Its underlying trading system is known as TradElect and there are a number of trading platforms that serve different sectors of the market.

The main trading system is SETS, which is used to trade shares that are contained within the FTSE All Share Index. It combines electronic order driven trading with integrated market maker liquidity provision, delivering guaranteed two-way prices for the most liquid and international securities.

In this system, LSE member firms (investment banks and brokers) input orders via computer terminals. These orders may be for the member firms themselves, or for their clients.

Very simply, the way the system operates is that these orders will be added to the 'buy queue' or the 'sell queue', or executed immediately. Investors who add their order to the relevant queue are prepared to hold out for the price they want. Those seeking immediate execution will trade against the queue of buyers (if they are selling) or against the sellers' queue (if they are buying).

The following is an example of a SETS screen:

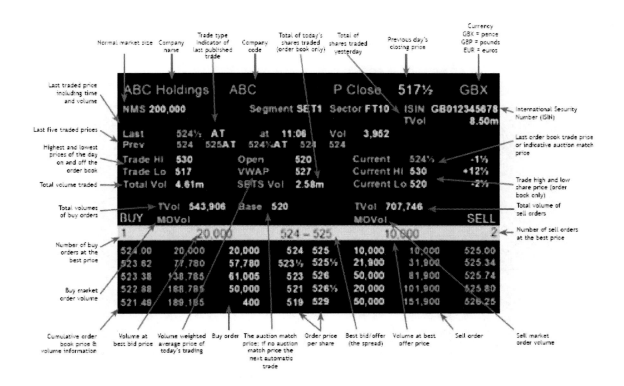

Source: London Stock Exchange

For a liquid stock, like Vodafone, there will be a 'deep' order book – the term 'deep' implies that there are lots of orders waiting to be dealt on either side. The top of the queues might look like this:

Buy Queue		Sell Queue	
We will buy for at least		**We will sell for at least**	
7,000 shares	£1.24	3,500 shares	£1.25
5,150 shares	£1.23	1,984 shares (2)	£1.26
19,250 shares (1)	£1.22	75,397 shares (2)	£1.26
44,000 shares (1)	£1.22	17,300 shares	£1.27

Queue priority is given on the basis of price and then time.

So, for the orders noted (1), the order to buy 19,250 shares must have been placed before the 44,000 order – hence its position higher up the queue. Similarly, for the orders noted (2), the order to sell 1,984 shares must have been input before the order to sell 75,397 shares.

Not all shares have sufficient liquidity to permit trading to take place and the London Stock Exchange has an alternative system for shares where the volume of shares traded is low. Less liquid securities that are not traded on the SETS order book are traded on SETSqx which stands for Stock Exchange Electronic Trading Service – quotes and crosses. It combines periodic auctions with quotes from market makers so that trading can take place throughout the trading day.

An example of a SETSqx screen is shown below.

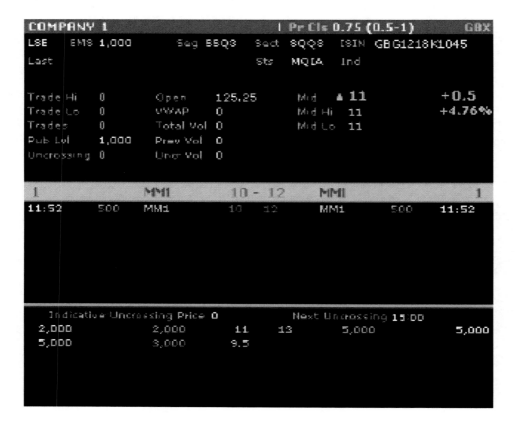

Source: London Stock Exchange

It is a quote-driven system with market makers providing liquidity during the trading day. The SETSqx yellow strip displays information regarding the current best bid and offer for the security based on the market maker quotes only. Where there is no registered market maker, the yellow strip will instead show the best bid and offer prices available.

Trading for the fixed interest market and any AIM securities that are not traded on either of the above platforms are traded using the quote-driven platform SEAQ.

SEAQ is an acronym for Stock Exchange Automated Quotation. Each stock has a page on which LSE member firms can display, if they wish, their 'quoted prices', the prices at which they are willing to buy (known as the 'bid prices'), the prices at which they are willing to sell (known as the 'offer prices') and the sizes of transaction in which they will do so.

The SEAQ screens can be thought of as advertisements of prices and quantities. Deals are done when a member firm reacts to the advertised prices and contacts the market maker by telephone. The market maker has to honour the prices and quantities that it is displaying on SEAQ.

9.   SETTLEMENT

LEARNING OBJECTIVES

4.1.12   Know the method of holding title – registered v bearer

9.1   Methods of Holding Title

Shares can be issued in either registered or bearer form.

Holding shares in registered form involves the investor's name being recorded on the share register and, often, being issued with a share certificate to reflect the person's ownership. However, many companies which issue registered shares now do so on a non-certificated basis.

The alternative to holding shares in registered form is to hold bearer shares. As the name suggests, the person who holds, or is the 'bearer' of, the shares is the owner. Ownership passes by transfer of the share certificate to the new owner.

This adds a degree of risk to holding shares in that loss of the certificate might equal loss of the person's investment. As a result, holding bearer shares is relatively rare, especially in the UK. In addition, bearer shares are regarded unfavourably by the regulatory authorities due to the opportunities they offer for money laundering. Consequently, they are usually immobilised in depositories such as Euroclear, or by their local country registries.

9.2   Certificated Shares

In all but a very few cases, a UK company is required to maintain a share register. This is simply a record of all current shareholders in that company, and how many shares they each hold. The share register is kept by the company registrar, who might be an employee of the company itself or a specialist firm of registrars.

When a shareholder sells some, or all, of his shareholding, there must be a mechanism for updating the register to reflect the buyer and effect the change of ownership and for transferring the money to the seller. This is required in order to settle the transaction – accordingly, it is described as 'settlement'.

Historically, each shareholder also held a share certificate as evidence of the shares they owned. When shares were sold, the seller sent their share certificate and a stock transfer form, providing details of the new owner, to the company registrar.

Acting on these documents, the registrar would delete the seller's name and insert the name of the buyer into the register. The registrar then issued a new certificate to the buyer. This was commonly referred to as 'certificated settlement' because the completion of a transaction required the issue of a new share certificate.

Certificated settlement is cumbersome and inefficient; over the past decade most UK settlement has moved to a paperless, dematerialised (or uncertificated) form of settlement through a system called CREST.

9.3   UK Settlement System – CREST

LEARNING OBJECTIVES

4.1.13   Understand the role played by Euroclear in the clearing and settlement of equity trades: uncertificated transfers, participants (members, payment banks, registrars)

9.3.1   Introduction

CREST is the central securities depository for UK and Irish equities.

It is a computer-based system operated by Euroclear UK and Ireland; some of its key features are:

- Holdings are uncertificated, that is, share certificates are not required to evidence transfer of ownership.
- There is real-time matching of trades.
- Settlement of transactions takes place in multiple currencies.
- Electronic transfer of title takes place on settlement.
- Settlement generates guaranteed obligations to pay cash outside CREST.
- Coverage includes shares, corporate and government bonds and other securities held in registered form.
- Processing of a range of corporate actions including dividend distributions and rights issues.

It started operating in 1996, replacing the Talisman system operated by the Stock Exchange and merged with Euroclear in September 2002.

9.3.2   Electronic Transfer of Title (ETT)

The Companies Act confers powers on the treasury to make regulations to enable title to securities to be evidenced and transferred without the need for a written instrument.

The legal framework for the CREST settlement system was implemented by the Uncertified Securities Regulations 1995. In 2001 further regulations eliminated the interval between settlement in CREST and transfer of legal title by entry on the share register, by introducing transfer of legal title at the point of electronic settlement, known as 'Electronic Transfer of Title' (ETT).

9.3.3 CREST Structure

Each CREST member has a participant ID and at least one member account ID. Shares of different companies are held within the member's account and allocated to separate securities accounts.

The securities accounts distinguish amounts that are available to settle outstanding transactions and amounts that are in deposit which are used to facilitate transfers of certificated shares.

CREST users input their instructions and receive information via one of the three electronic networks operated by Syntegra, SWIFT and the LSE. Users are able to communicate with CREST only through the network and do not communicate directly with one another.

9.3.4 Holding Securities in CREST

Shares in CREST are held in an uncertificated form in one of the following three ways:

- **Direct Member** – involves the member's name appearing on the issuing company's register. Each member has a stock account containing records of its securities and each appoints a CREST payment bank to pay out and receive moneys in respect of CREST transactions. Direct members are permitted to hold more than one account, to facilitate designation of accounts (for example, for different underlying clients).
- **Sponsored Members** – are generally private investors and their name will appear on the issuing company's register. A direct member will act as their sponsor to provide the link to CREST and is typically a broker, fund manager or custodian who charges a fee for the service. A sponsored member is also required to appoint a CREST payment bank.
- **Custodian** – where the beneficial shareholder appoints a nominee who is a direct member of CREST. The nominee holds the securities on behalf of the shareholder, through a specially designated stock account. The nominee company's name appears on the issuing company's share register, as opposed to the shareholder's name. The nominee company is typically operated by a broker, fund manager or custodian.

9.3.5 Payment Banks and Cash Memorandum Accounts

As mentioned above, CREST members are required to appoint a CREST payment bank to receive and pay out monies in respect of settlements in CREST.

CREST maintains one or more Cash Memorandum Accounts (CMAs) for each member in one or more CREST settlements currencies (eg, euro, sterling or US dollars) as required by the member. A CMA is an electronic transaction ledger which shows the net balance of payments made and received at any time during the course of the settlement day.

Settlement is instantaneous and payments are made between settlement banks on the central accounts at the Bank of England as they occur.

9.3.6   Transfers and Registers of Title

Under the CREST system, the 'register' of securities comprises two parts:

- CREST maintains the uncertificated part of the register – the Operator Register of Securities.
- The relevant issuer maintains the certificated part of the register – the Issuer Register of Securities.

When any transfer of title occurs in CREST, the CREST system will generate a Register Update Request (RUR) requiring the issuer to amend the relevant record of uncertificated shares.

The Issuer Register of Uncertificated Securities is simply a duplicate of the CREST register but the combination of this and the issuer's register of certificated securities means that the issuer is aware of, and can communicate with, all the holders of its securities.

9.3.7   Settlement in CREST

The diagram below illustrates how a sterling sale of UK-registered shares between two counterparties on a recognised exchange is input, matched and settled in CREST.

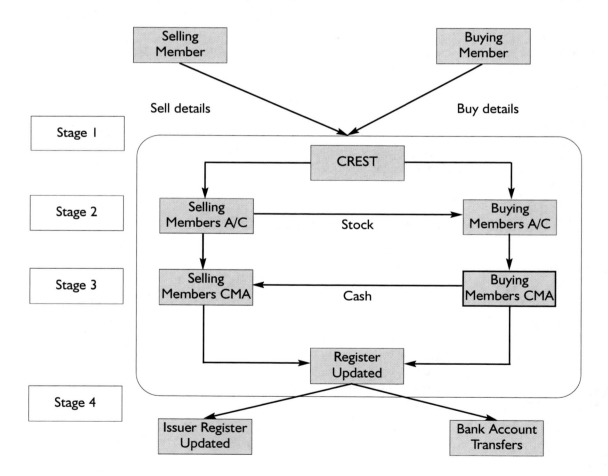

Stage 1 – Trade Matching

- The buying and selling members input instructions in CREST detailing the terms of the agreed trade.
- CREST authenticates these instructions to check that they conform to the authentication procedures stipulated by CREST. If the input data from both members is identical, CREST creates a matching transaction.

Stage 2 – Stock Settlement

- On the intended settlement date, CREST checks that the buying member has the funds, the selling member has sufficient stock in its stock account and the buyer's CREST settlement bank has sufficient liquidity at the Bank of England to proceed to settlement of the transaction.
- If so, CREST moves the stock from the selling member's account to the buying member's account.

Stage 3 – Cash Settlement

- CREST also credits the CMA of the selling member and debits the CMA of the buying member which simultaneously generates a settlement bank payment obligation of the buying member's settlement bank in favour of the Bank of England.
- The selling member's settlement bank receives that payment in Bank of England funds immediately upon the debit of the purchase price to the buying member's CMA.

Stage 4 – Register Update

- CREST then automatically updates its Operator Register of Securities to effect the transfer of shares to the buying member.
- Legal title to the shares passes at this point – Electronic Transfer of Title (ETT), as described earlier.
- This prompts the simultaneous generation by the CREST system of a RUR requiring the issuer to amend its record of uncertificated shares.

In practice, stages 2, 3 and 4 occur simultaneously.

9.3.8 Holding of Securities in Certificated Form

If a member of CREST sells securities in certificated form, the member or his broker will deposit a CREST transfer form and the relevant share certificate at one of four regional CREST counters and input an electronic CREST record.

The transfer form and certificate are processed and transferred to the appropriate registrar. The registrar will check the documents and delete securities registered in the name of the transferor from the register and ensure that the securities are credited to the CREST membership of the buyer as specified in the transfer form. The buyer thereby obtains title to the securities in electronic form.

Similarly, if a member purchases and receives securities in electronic form but wishes to hold them in certificated form, when the seller receives the purchase funds he will instruct CREST to remove the securities from his register and instruct the registrar, through CREST, to register the securities in the name of the purchaser. The registrar will then produce a certificate in the purchaser's name.

END OF CHAPTER QUESTIONS

Think of an answer for each question and refer to the appropriate section for confirmation.

Question	Answer Reference
1. What are the constitutional documents of a company more commonly known as?	Section 2.1
2. When a shareholder appoints someone to vote on his behalf at a company meeting, what it is referred to as?	Sections 2.3 & 5.5
3. Which body is responsible for approving the listing of companies on the London Stock Exchange?	Section 3.2
4. What are the features of a cumulative preference share?	Section 4.2
5. Why might a company have a higher than average dividend yield?	Section 5.1
6. What options are available to an investor in a rights issue?	Section 7.1
7. Under what type of corporate action would an investor receive additional shares without making any payment?	Section 7.2
8. What is the key characteristic of an order-driven trading system?	Section 8
9. AIM shares are traded on which London Stock Exchange system?	Section 8
10. What is ETT?	Section 9.3.2

CHAPTER FIVE

BONDS

This syllabus area will provide approximately 4 of the 50 examination questions

Although bonds rarely generate as much attention as shares, they are the larger market of the two in terms of global investment value.

Bonds are roughly equally split between 'government' and 'corporate' bonds. Government bonds are issued by national governments and by supra national agencies, such as the European Investment Bank and the World Bank. Corporate bonds are issued by companies, such as the large banks and other large corporate listed companies.

In this chapter, we will firstly look at the common characteristics of bonds and then consider the key features of both government and corporate bonds.

1. CHARACTERISTICS OF BONDS

LEARNING OBJECTIVES

5.1.1   Know the definition and features of government bonds: DMO maturity classifications; how they are issued

A bond is, very simply, a loan.

A company that needs to raise money to finance an investment could borrow money from their bank, or alternatively, they could issue a bond to raise the funds they need. With a bond, an investor lends in return for the promise to have the loan repaid on a fixed date and (usually) a series of interest payments.

Bonds are commonly referred to as loan stock, debt and (in the case of those which pay fixed income) fixed interest securities.

The feature that distinguishes a bond from any other kind of loan is that a bond is tradable. Investors can buy and sell bonds without the need to refer to the original borrower.

Although there are a wide variety of fixed interest securities in issue, they all share similar characteristics. These can be described by looking at an example of a UK government bond and explaining what each of the terms means.

To explain the terminology associated with bonds, we will assume that an investor has purchased a holding of £10,000 nominal of 5% treasury stock 2012. The convention in the bond markets is to quote the prices of bonds per £100 nominal, so if the stock is currently priced at £101.25, then the holding has a market value of £10,125.00, that is, the nominal value of £10,000 multiplied by the price of £101.25.

Nominal[1]	Stock[2]	Price[5]	Value[6]
£10,000	5%[3] Treasury Stock 2012[4]	£101.25	£10,125.00

Each of the terms annotated above is explained below:

1. **Nominal** – This is the amount of stock purchased and should not be confused with the amount invested or the cost of purchase. This is the amount on which interest will be paid and what will eventually be repaid.
2. **Stock** – Name given to identify the stock.
3. **5%** – This is the nominal interest rate payable on the stock, also known as the coupon. The rate is quoted gross and will normally be paid in two separate and equal half-yearly interest payments. The annual amount of interest paid is calculated by multiplying the nominal amount of stock held by the coupon; that is, in this case, £10,000 times 5%.
4. **2012** – This is the year in which the stock will be repaid. Repayment will take place at the same time as the final interest payment is made. The amount repaid will be the nominal amount of stock held; that is, £10,000.
5. **Price** – The convention in the bond markets is to quote prices per £100 nominal of stock. So, in this example, the price is £101.25 for each £100 nominal of stock.
6. **Value** – The value of the stock is calculated by multiplying the nominal amount of stock by the current price.

EXAMPLE

Gilts are named by their coupon rate and their redemption date, for example, 6% treasury stock 2028.

The coupon indicates the cash payment per £100 nominal value that the holder will receive each year (unless tax is deducted at source). This interest payment is usually made in two equal semi-annual payments on fixed dates, six months apart.

An investor holding £1,000 nominal of 6% treasury stock 2028 will receive two coupon payments of £30 each, on 7 June and 7 December each year, until the repayment of £1,000 on 7 December 2028.

2. GOVERNMENT BONDS

LEARNING OBJECTIVES

5.1.1 Know the definition and features of government bonds: DMO maturity classifications, how they are issued

Governments issue bonds to finance their spending and investment plans and to bridge the gap between their actual spending and the tax and other forms of income that they receive. Issuance of bonds is high when tax revenues are significantly less than government spending.

Western governments are major borrowers of money, so the volume of government bonds in issue is very large and forms a major part of the investment portfolio of many institutional investors (like pension funds and insurance companies).

The main types of government bonds that are in issue can be classified as follows:

- conventional;
- dual-dated;
- index-linked; and
- irredeemable.

2.1   Conventional Bonds

Conventional government bonds are instruments that carry a fixed coupon and a single repayment date, such as in the example used above of 5% treasury stock 2012.

This type of bond represents the majority of government bonds in issue.

2.2   Dual-Dated Bonds

These types of bonds will carry a fixed coupon but show two dates, between which they can be repaid. The decision as to when to repay will be made by the government and will depend on the prevailing rates of interest at that time.

An example of this is 7¾% treasury loan 2012–15. In this case, the government must repay the stock in full by 2015 but has the option to do so earlier, starting in 2012. If the government can issue new bonds carrying a coupon of less than 7¾% then it can save money by repaying the bond earlier and refinancing it with another bond at a lower rate of interest. If interest rates are higher, it will not have any incentive to do so and will wait until the final redemption date.

Bonds such as these are attractive to governments as they give them flexibility to manage the country's finances. By contrast, they are not as attractive to investors as on repayment they may be able to reinvest the proceeds only at a lower rate of interest.

2.3   Index-Linked Bonds

Index-linked bonds are ones where the coupon and the redemption amount are increased by the amount of inflation over the life of the bond.

An example is 2½% treasury index-linked stock 2020. When this stock was issued, it carried a coupon of 2½% but this is uplifted by the amount of inflation at each interest payment. Similarly, the amount that will be repaid in 2020 is adjusted.

Index-linked bonds are attractive in periods where a government's control of inflation is uncertain by providing extra protection to the investor.

They are also attractive to long-term investors such as pension funds. They need to invest their funds and know that the returns will maintain their real value after inflation so that they can meet their obligations to pay pensions.

2.4   Irredeemable Bonds

There are a limited number of government stocks which are irredeemable; that is, they have no fixed repayment date. They are also called perpetual stocks or undated stocks, because they have no set date for the nominal value to be repaid.

An example is 3½% War Stock which was issued to fund government expenditure during the Second World War and which is still in issue.

Needless to say, the lack of a certain repayment date is unattractive to investors. However, there is a sinking fund, by way of which the government repays a certain amount of its undated stock (selected by ballot).

2.5   Classifications

As well as categorising government bonds by type, another common division is by duration.

Generally, short-term debt is considered to be one year or less, long-term is more than ten years. Medium-term debt falls somewhere in the middle.

The actual classifications change, however, by market. As an example, UK government stocks are classified in terms of the number of years that remain until the nominal value is repaid:

* 0–7 years remaining   –   short-dated;
* 7–15 years remaining   –   medium-dated;
* 15 years and over remaining   –   long-dated.

In 2005, the UK Debt Management Office (DMO) issued new gilts with redemption dates of over 50 years for the first time. Although these are classified within the banding of 15 years and over, they are referred to as 'ultra-long' gilts.

2.6   Primary Market Issuance

Government bonds are usually issued through agencies that are part of that country's treasury department.

In the UK, for example, when a new gilt is issued, the process is handled by the Debt Management Office (DMO) which is an agency acting on behalf of the treasury.

Issues are typically made in the form of an auction, where large investors (such as banks, pension funds and insurance companies) submit competitive bids. Often they will each bid for several million pounds' worth of an issue. Issue amounts are normally between £0.5 billion and £2 billion. The DMO accepts bids from those prepared to pay the highest price.

Smaller investors are able to submit non-competitive bids. Advertisements in the Financial Times and other newspapers will include details of the offer and an application form. Non-competitive bids can be submitted for up to £500,000, and the applicant will pay the average of the prices paid by competitive bidders.

3. CORPORATE BONDS

A corporate bond is a bond that is issued by a company, as the name suggests.

The term is usually applied to longer-term debt instruments, with a maturity date of more than 12 months. The term commercial paper is used for instruments with a shorter maturity. Only companies with high credit ratings can issue bonds with a maturity greater than ten years at an acceptable cost.

Most corporate bonds are listed on stock exchanges but the majority of trading in most developed markets takes place in the OTC market.

3.1   Features of Corporate Bonds

There are a wide variety of corporate bonds and they can often be differentiated by looking at some of their key features, such as:

* security; and
* redemption provisions.

3.1.1 Bond Security

When a company is seeking to raise new funds by way of a bond issue, it will often have to offer 'security' to provide the investor with some guarantee for the repayment of the bond. In this context, security usually means some form of charge over the issuer's assets (eg, its property or trade assets) so that if the issuer defaults, the bondholders have a claim on those assets before other creditors (and so can regard their borrowings as safer than if there were no security).

In some cases, the security takes the form of a third party guarantee – for example, a guarantee by a bank that if the issuer defaults, the bank will repay the bondholders.

The greater the security offered, then the lower the cost of borrowing should be.

The security offered may be fixed or floating. Fixed security implies that specific assets (eg, a building) of the company are charged as security for the loan. A floating charge means that the general assets of the company are offered as security for the loan; this might include cash at the bank, trade debtors, stock and the like.

3.1.2   Redemption Provisions

In some cases, a corporate bond will have a call provision which gives the issuer the option to buy back all or part of the issue before maturity.

This is attractive to the issuer as it gives it the option to refinance the bond (ie, replace it with one at a lower rate of interest) when interest rates are lower than what is being paid. This is a disadvantage, however, to the investor who will probably demand a higher yield as compensation.

Call provisions can take various forms. There may be a requirement for the issuer to redeem a specified amount at regular intervals. This is known as a 'sinking fund' requirement.

You may also see bonds with 'put' provisions, known as 'puttable' bonds. These give the bondholder the right to require the issuer to redeem early, on a set date or between specific dates. This makes the bond attractive to borrowers and may increase the chances of selling a bond issue in the first instance; it does, however, increase the issuer's risk that it will have to refinance the bond at an inconvenient time.

3.2   Domestic Bonds

The development of financial engineering techniques in banks around the world has resulted in a large variety of corporate debt being issued and traded. Some of the main types are described below.

3.2.1   Medium-Term Notes

Medium-term notes are standard corporate bonds with maturities ranging usually from nine months to five years; though the term is also applied to instruments with maturities as long as 30 years. Where they differ from other debt instruments is that they are offered to investors continually over a period of time by an agent of the issuer, instead of in a single tranche of one, sizeable, underwritten issue.

The market originated in the US to close the funding gap between commercial paper and long-term bonds.

3.2.2   Fixed Rate Bonds

The key features of fixed rate bonds have already been described in Section 1. Essentially, they have fixed coupons which are paid either half-yearly or annually and predetermined redemption dates.

3.2.3   Floating Rate Notes

Floating Rate Notes are usually referred to as FRNs and are bonds that have variable rates of interest.

The rate of interest will be linked to a benchmark rate, such as, the London InterBank Offered Rate (LIBOR). This is the rate of interest at which banks will lend to one another in London, and is often used as a basis for financial instrument cash flows.

An FRN will usually pay interest at LIBOR plus a quoted margin or spread.

3.2.4 Permanent Interest Bearing Shares (PIBS)

PIBS are a type of instrument that is peculiar to the UK sterling market. The term stands for Permanent Interest Bearing Shares and they are issued by building societies. They carry fixed coupons and are irredeemable.

We will look separately at some other types of bonds in the following sections.

3.2.5 Convertible Bonds

Convertible bonds are issued by companies. They give the investor holding the bond two possible choices:

- to simply collect the interest payments and then the repayment of the bond on maturity; or
- to convert the bond into a predefined number of ordinary shares in the issuing company, on a set date or dates, or between a range of set dates, prior to the bond's maturity.

The attractions to the investor are:

- If the company prospers, its share price will rise and, if it does so sufficiently, conversion may lead to capital gains.
- If the company hits problems, the investor will retain the bond – interest will be earned and, as bondholders, the investor would rank ahead of existing shareholders if the company goes bust. (Of course, if the company was seriously insolvent and the bond was unsecured, the bondholder might still not be repaid – but this is a remoter possibility than that of a full loss as a shareholder.)

For the company, relatively cheap finance is acquired. Investors will pay a higher price for a bond that is convertible because of the possibility of a capital gain. However, the prospect of dilution of current shareholder interests, as convertible bondholders exercise their options, has to be borne in mind.

3.3 Foreign Bonds

Bonds can be categorised geographically. A domestic bond is issued by a domestic issuer into the domestic market, for example, a UK company issuing bonds, denominated in sterling, to UK investors.

In contrast, a foreign bond is issued by an overseas entity, into a domestic market and is denominated in the domestic currency. Examples of a foreign bond are a German company issuing a sterling bond to UK investors, or a US dollar bond issued in the US by a non-US company.

3.4 Eurobonds

Eurobonds are large international bond issues often made by governments and multinational companies.

The eurobond market developed in the early 1970s to accommodate the recycling of substantial OPEC US dollar revenues from Middle East oil sales at a time when US financial institutions were subject to a ceiling on the rate of interest that could be paid on dollar deposits. Since then it has grown exponentially into the world's largest market for longer-term capital, as a result of the corresponding growth in world trade and even more significant growth in international capital flows, with most of the activity being concentrated in London.

Often issued in a number of financial centres simultaneously, the defining characteristic of eurobonds is that they are denominated in a currency different from that of the financial centre or centres in which they are issued.

In this respect, the term eurobond is a bit of a misnomer as eurobond issues, and the currencies in which they are denominated, are not restricted to those of European financial centres or countries.

The 'euro' prefix simply originates from the depositing of US dollars in the European eurodollar market and has been applied to the eurobond market since. So, a euro Sterling bond issue is one denominated in Sterling and issued outside the UK, though not necessarily in a european financial centre.

Eurobonds issued by companies often do not provide any underlying collateral, or security, to the bondholders but are almost always credit rated by a credit rating agency.

To prevent the interests of these bondholders being subordinated, or made inferior, to those of any subsequent bond issues, the company makes a 'negative pledge' clause. This prevents the company from subsequently making any secured bond issues, or issues which confer greater seniority (ie, priority) or entitlement to the company's assets, in the event of its liquidation, unless an equivalent level of security is provided to existing bondholders.

The eurobond market offers a number of advantages over a domestic bond market, making it attractive for companies to raise capital, including:

* a choice of innovative products to more exactly meet issuers' needs;
* the ability to reach potential lenders internationally rather than just domestically;
* anonymity to investors as issues are made in bearer form;
* gross interest payments to investors;
* lower funding costs due to the competitive nature and greater liquidity of the market;
* the ability to make bond issues at short notice; and
* less regulation and disclosure.

Most eurobonds are issued as conventional bonds (or 'straights'), with a fixed nominal value, fixed coupon and known redemption date. Other common types include floating rate notes, zero coupon bonds, convertible bonds and dual-currency bonds – but they can also assume a wide range of other innovative features.

3.5   Asset-Backed Securities

There is a large group of bonds that trade under the overall heading of 'asset-backed securities'.

These are bundled securities, so called because they are marketable securities that result from the bundling or packaging together of a set of non-marketable assets.

The assets in this pool, or bundle, range from mortgages and credit card debt to accounts receivable. The largest market is for mortgage-backed securities whose cash flows are backed by the principal and interest payments of a set of mortgages. These have become known worldwide as a result of the sub-prime collapse in the US – where concerns over the poor quality of the underlying mortgages caused a collapse in the price of mortgage-backed bonds.

A significant advantage of asset-backed securities is that they bring together a pool of financial assets that otherwise could not easily be traded in their existing form. By pooling together a large portfolio of these illiquid assets they can be converted into instruments that may be offered and sold freely in the capital markets.

3.6 Zero Coupon Bond (ZCB)

A zero coupon bond (ZCB) is a bond that pays no interest. 'Coupon' is an alternative term for the interest payment on a bond.

EXAMPLE

Imagine the issuer of a bond (example plc) offered you the opportunity to purchase a bond with the following features:

- £100 nominal value.

- Issued today.

- Redeems at its par value (that is £100 nominal value) in five years.

- Pays no interest.

Would you be interested in purchasing the bond? It is tempting to say no – who would want to buy a bond that pays no interest? However, there is no requirement to pay the par value – a logical investor would presumably happily pay something less than the par value, for example £60. The difference between the price the investor paid of £60 and the par value of £100 recouped after five years would provide the investor with his return of £40 over five years.

As the example illustrates, these zero coupon bonds are issued at a discount to their par value and repay, or redeem, at par value. All of the return is provided in the form of capital growth rather than income and, as a result, is treated differently for tax purposes.

4. INVESTING IN BONDS

LEARNING OBJECTIVES

5.3.1   Know the advantages and disadvantages of investing in different types
         of bonds

4.1   Advantages and Disadvantages of Investing

As one of the main asset classes, bonds clearly have a role to play in most portfolios.

Their main advantages are:

- For fixed-interest bonds, a regular and certain flow of income.
- For most bonds, a fixed maturity date (but there are bonds which have no redemption date, and others which may be repaid on either of two dates or between two dates – some at the investor's option and some at the issuer's option).
- A range of income yields to suit different investment and tax situations.

Their main disadvantages are:

- The 'real' value of the income flow is eroded by the effects of inflation (except in the case of index-linked bonds).
- Default risk, namely that the issuer will not be able to make interest payments as they fall due or repay the capital at the maturity date.

As can be seen, there are a number of risks attached to holding bonds.

Bonds generally have default risk (the company could go bust) and price risk. Most government bonds have only price risk as there is little or no risk that the government will fail to pay the interest or repay the capital on the bonds.

Price or market risk is of particular concern to bondholders who are open to the effect of movements in interest rates, which can have a significant impact on the value of their holdings.

This is best explained by two simple examples.

EXAMPLE

Interest rates are approximately 5%, and the government issues a bond with a coupon rate of 5% interest. Three months later interest rates have doubled to 10%. What will happen to the value of the bond? The value of the bond will fall substantially. Its 5% interest is no longer attractive, so its resale price will fall to compensate and make the return it offers more competitive.

EXAMPLE

Interest rates are approximately 5%, and the government issues a bond with a coupon rate of 5% interest. Interest rates generally have fallen to 2.5%. What will happen to the value of the bond? The value of the bond will rise substantially. Its 5% interest is very attractive, so its resale price will rise to compensate and make the return it offers fall to more realistic levels.

With both of these examples, remember that it is the current value of the bond that is changing. Changes in interest rates do not affect the amount payable at maturity, which will remain as the nominal amount of the stock.

As the above examples illustrate, there is an inverse relationship between interest rates and bond prices:

- If interest rates increase, bond prices will decrease.
- If interest rates decrease, bond prices will increase.

Some of the other main risks associated with holding bonds are:

- **Early redemption** – the risk that the issuer may invoke a call provision (if the bond is callable).
- **Seniority risk** – the seniority with which corporate debt is ranked in the event of the issuer's liquidation. Debt with the highest seniority is repaid first in the event of liquidation; so debt with the highest seniority has a greater chance of being repaid than debt with lower seniority.
- **Inflation risk** – the risk of inflation rising unexpectedly and eroding the real value of the bond's coupon and redemption payment.
- **Liquidity risk** – liquidity is the ease with which a security can be converted into cash. Some bonds are more easily sold at a fair market price than others.
- **Exchange rate risk** – bonds denominated in a currency different to that of the investor's home currency are potentially subject to adverse exchange rate movements.
- **Default risk** – refers to the possibility of an issuer defaulting on the payment of interest or capital.

4.2   Flat Yields

LEARNING OBJECTIVES

5.3.2   Be able to calculate the flat yield of a bond

Yields are a measure of the returns to be earned on bonds.

The coupon reflects the interest rate payable on the nominal or principal amount. However, an investor will have paid a different amount to purchase the bond, so a method of calculating the true return to him is needed.

The return, as a percentage of the cost price, which a bond offers is often referred to as the bond's 'yield'. The interest paid on a bond as a percentage of its market price is referred to as the 'flat', or 'running', yield.

The flat yield is calculated by taking the annual coupon and dividing by the bond's price and then multiplying by 100 to obtain a percentage. The bond's price is typically stated as the price payable to purchase £100 nominal value. This is best illustrated by looking at the following examples:

EXAMPLE

A bond with a coupon of 5%, issued by **XYZ plc**, redeemable in 2012, is currently trading at £100 per £100 nominal.

The flat yield is the coupon divided by the price expressed as a percentage, ie:

£5/£100 x 100 = 5%.

EXAMPLE

A bond with a coupon of 4%, issued by **ABC plc**, redeemable in 2020, is currently trading at £78 per £100 nominal. So an investor could buy £100 nominal value for £78.

The flat yield is the coupon divided by the price expressed as a percentage, ie:

£4/£78 x 100 = 5.13%.

EXAMPLE

5% Treasury Stock 2028 is currently priced at £104. So an investor could buy £100 nominal value for £104.

The flat yield on this gilt is the coupon divided by the price, ie:

£5/£104 x 100 = 4.81%.

4.3 Rating Agencies

LEARNING OBJECTIVES

5.3.3   Understand the role of credit rating agencies and the differences between investment and non-investment grades

---

Credit risk, or the probability of an issuer defaulting on their payment obligations and the extent of the resulting loss, can be assessed by reference to the independent credit ratings given to most bond issues.

The three most prominent credit rating agencies that provide these ratings are:

- Standard & Poor's;
- Moody's; and
- Fitch Ratings.

Bond issues subject to credit ratings can be divided into two distinct categories: those accorded an 'investment grade' rating and those categorised as non-investment grade or speculative. The latter are also known as 'high yield' or, for the worst rated, 'junk bonds'. Investment grade issues offer the greatest liquidity and certainty of repayment.

Bonds will be assessed and given a credit rating when they are first issued and then re-assessed if circumstances change so that their rating can be upgraded or downgraded with a consequent effect on their price.

HOTSPOT

5

Go online to your elearning product for further information on bonds.

If you haven't purchased your elearning product, you can order now by calling Client Services on +44(0)20 7645 0680.

END OF CHAPTER QUESTIONS

Think of an answer for each question and refer to the appropriate section for confirmation.

Question	Answer Reference
1. 5% Treasury Stock 2012 is an example of what type of government bond?	Section 2.1
2. Which type of government bond would you expect to be most attractive during a period of rising inflation?	Section 2.3
3. What is the function of a call provision when attached to a bond?	Section 3.1.2
4. What is the typical maturity period for a medium-term note?	Section 3.2.1
5. What options does a convertible bond give to an investor?	Section 3.2.5
6. What types of assets might you see pooled together to provide the backing for an asset-backed security?	Section 3.5
7. What type of bond does not pay interest?	Section 3.6
8. What will be the impact of a fall in interest rates on bond prices?	Section 4.1
9. You have a holding of £1000 Treasury 5% Stock 2028 which is priced at 104. What is its flat yield?	Section 4.2
10. What credit rating should be looked for in a bond when seeking the greatest liquidity and certainty of repayment.	Section 4.3

DERIVATIVES

This syllabus area will provide approximately 3 of the 50 examination questions

1.   USES OF DERIVATIVES

LEARNING OBJECTIVES

6.1.1   Understand the uses and application of derivatives

A derivative is a financial instrument whose value is based on the price of an underlying asset.

This underlying asset could be a financial asset, such as those considered in the previous chapters, or a commodity – examples include bonds, shares, stock market indices and interest rates; for commodities they include oil, silver or wheat.

Derivatives have a major role to play in the investment management of many large portfolios and funds and are used for hedging, anticipating future cash flows, asset allocation change and arbitrage.

Hedging is a technique employed by portfolio managers to reduce the impact of adverse price movements by selling sufficient futures contracts.

Closely linked to this idea, if a portfolio manager expects to receive a large inflow of cash to be invested in a particular asset, then futures can be used to fix the price at which it will be bought and offset the risk that prices will have risen by the time the cash flow is received.

Changes to the asset allocation of a fund, whether to take advantage of anticipated short-term directional market movements or to implement a change in strategy, can be made more swiftly and less expensively using futures than by adjusting the underlying portfolio.

Arbitrage is the process of deriving a risk-free profit from simultaneously buying and selling the same asset in two different markets, where a price difference between the two exists. If the price of a derivative and its underlying asset are mismatched, then the portfolio manager may be able to profit from this pricing anomaly.

2.   FUTURES

LEARNING OBJECTIVES

6.2.1   Know the definition and function of a future

6.4.1   Understand the following terms: long, short, open, close, holder,
          writing, premium, covered, naked, OTC, exchange-traded

2.1   Development of Futures

Derivatives are not a new concept and, in fact, have been around for hundreds of years. Their origins
can be traced back to agricultural markets where farmers needed a mechanism to guard against price
fluctuations caused by gluts of produce and drought. So, in order to fix the price of agricultural produce
in advance of harvest time, farmers and merchants entered into forward contracts. These set the
price at which a stated amount of a commodity would be delivered between a farmer and a merchant
(termed the 'counterparties'), at a prespecified future time.

These early derivative contracts introduced an element of certainty into commerce and gained
immense popularity; they led to the opening of the world's first derivatives exchange, the Chicago
Board of Trade (CBOT), in 1848.

The exchange soon developed a futures contract that enabled standardised qualities and quantities of
grain to be traded for a fixed future price on a stated delivery date. Unlike the forward contracts that
preceded it, the futures contract could itself be traded. These futures contracts were subsequently
extended to a wide variety of commodities and offered by an ever-increasing number of derivatives
exchanges.

It wasn't until 1975 that CBOT introduced the world's first financial futures contract. This set the scene
for the exponential growth in product innovation and the volume of futures trading that soon followed.

2.2   Futures

Derivatives provide a mechanism by which the price of assets or commodities can be traded in the
future at a price agreed today without the full value of this transaction being exchanged or settled at
the outset. future is an agreement between a buyer and a seller. The buyer agrees to pay a prespecified
amount for the delivery of a particular quantity of an asset at a future date. The seller agrees to deliver
the asset at the future date, in exchange for the prespecified amount of money.

EXAMPLE

A buyer might agree with a seller to pay $50 per barrel for 1,000 barrels of crude oil in three months.

**The buyer might be an electricity-generating company wanting to fix the price it will have to pay for
the oil to use in its oil-fired power stations and the seller might be an oil company wanting to fix the
sales price of some of its future oil production.**

2.3   Definition

A futures contract is a legally binding obligation between two parties for one to buy and the other to sell a prespecified amount of an asset at a prespecified price on a prespecified future date.

A futures contract has two distinct features:

- It is exchange-traded – for example, on the derivatives exchanges such as NYSE Liffe or the IntercontinentalExchange (ICE).
- It is dealt on standardised terms – the exchange specifies the quality of the underlying asset, the quantity underlying each contract, the future date and the delivery location – only the price is open to negotiation. In the above example, the oil quality will be based on the oil field from which it originates (eg, Brent crude – from the Brent oil field in the North Sea), the quantity is 1,000 barrels, the date is three months ahead and the location might be the port of Rotterdam.

2.4   Futures Terminology

Derivatives markets have specialised terminology that is important to understand.

Staying with the example above, the buyer of the contract to purchase 1,000 barrels of crude oil at $50 per barrel for delivery in three months is said to go 'long' of the contract, while the seller is described as going 'short'. Entering into the transaction is known as 'opening the trade'.

The definition of the terms that the futures market uses are as follows:

- **Long** – the term used for the position taken by the buyer of the future. The person who is 'long' of the contract is committed to buying the underlying asset at the pre-agreed price on the specified future date.
- **Short** – the position taken by the seller of the future. The seller is committed to delivering the underlying asset in exchange for the pre-agreed price on the specified future date.
- **Open** – the initial trade. A market participant opens a trade when it first enters into a future. It could be buying a future (opening a long position), or selling a future (opening a short position).
- **Close** – the physical assets underlying most futures that are opened do not end up being delivered: they are closed-out instead. For example, an opening buyer will almost invariably avoid delivery by making a closing sale before the delivery date. If the buyer does not close-out, he will pay over the agreed sum and receive the underlying asset. This might be something the buyer is keen to avoid, for example, because the buyer is actually a financial institution simply speculating on the price of the underlying asset using futures.
- **Covered** – is where the seller of the future has the underlying asset that will be needed if physical delivery takes place.
- **Naked** – is where the seller of the future does not have the asset that will be needed if physical delivery of the underlying commodity is required.

3.   OPTIONS

LEARNING OBJECTIVES

6.1.1   Know the differences between the major types of derivatives

6.3.1   Know the definition and function of an option

6.3.2   Understand the following terms: calls, puts

3.1   Development of Options

We now move on to consider options contracts. Options did not really start to flourish until two US academics produced an option pricing model in 1973 that allowed them to be readily priced. This paved the way for the creation of standardised options contracts and the opening of the Chicago Board Options Exchange (CBOE) in the same year. This in turn led to an explosion in product innovation and the creation of other option exchanges, such as NYSE Liffe.

Where options are traded on an exchange, they will be in standardised sizes and terms. From time to time, however, investors may wish to trade an option that is outside these standardised terms and they will do so in the over-the-counter (OTC) market. Options can therefore also be traded off-exchange, or OTC, where the contract specification determined by the parties is bespoke.

3.2   Options Definition

An option gives a buyer the right, but not the obligation, to buy or sell a specified quantity of an underlying asset at a pre-agreed exercise price, on or before a prespecified future date or between two specified dates. The seller, in exchange for the payment of a premium, grants the option to the buyer.

For exchange-traded contracts, both buyers and sellers contract with the exchange rather than with each other.

3.3   Options Terms

There are two classes of options:

*   A call option is where the buyer has the right to buy the asset at the exercise price, if he chooses to. The seller is obliged to deliver if the buyer exercises the option.
*   A put option is where the buyer has the right to sell the underlying asset at the exercise price. The seller of the put option is obliged to take delivery and pay the exercise price, if the buyer exercises the option.

Note: The buyers of options are the owners of those options. They are also referred to as holders.

The sellers of options are referred to as the 'writers' of those options. Their sale is also referred to as 'taking for the call' or 'taking for the put', depending on whether they receive a premium for selling a call option or a put option.

The exchange needs to be able to settle bargains if holders choose to exercise their rights to buy or sell. Since the exchange does not want to be a buyer or seller of the underlying asset, it matches these transactions with deals placed by the option writers who have agreed to deliver or receive the matching underlying asset, if called upon to do so.

The premium is the money paid by the buyer to the exchange (and then by the exchange to the writer) at the beginning of the option contract; it is not refundable.

The following example of an options contract is intended to assist in understanding the way in which option contracts might be used.

EXAMPLE

Suppose shares in Jersey plc are trading at 324p and an investor buys a 350p call for three months. The investor, Frank, has the right to buy Jersey shares from the writer of the option (another investor – Steve) at 350p if he chooses, at any stage over the next three months.

If Jersey shares are below 350p three months later, Frank will abandon the option.

If they rise to, say, 600p Frank will contact Steve and either:

*   exercise the option (buy the shares at 350p and keep them, or sell them at 600p); or

*   persuade Steve to give him 600 – 350p = 250p to settle the transaction.

If Frank paid a premium of 42p to Steve, what is Frank's maximum loss and what level does Jersey plc have to reach for Frank to make a profit?

The most Frank can lose is 42p, the premium he has paid. If the Jersey plc shares rise above 350 + 42p, or 392p, then he makes a profit. If the shares rise to 351p then Frank would exercise his right to buy – better to make a penny and cut his losses to 41p than lose the whole 42p.

HOTSPOT

6

Go online to your elearning product for further information on options.

If you haven't purchased your elearning product, you can order now by calling Client Services on +44(0)20 7645 0680.

---

4.   SWAPS

LEARNING OBJECTIVES

6.1.1   Know the differences between the major types of derivatives

6.5.1   Know the definition and function of an interest rate swap

4.1   Description of Swaps

A swap is an agreement to exchange one set of cash flows for another. They are most commonly used to switch financing from one currency to another or to replace floating interest with fixed interest.

Swaps are a form of OTC derivative and are negotiated between the parties to meet the different needs of customers, so each tends to be unique.

4.2   Interest Rate Swaps

Interest rate swaps are the most common form of swaps.

They involve an exchange of interest payments and are usually constructed whereby one leg of the swap is a payment of a fixed rate of interest and the other leg is a payment of a floating rate of interest.

They are usually used to hedge exposure to interest rate changes and can be easily appreciated by looking at an example.

EXAMPLE

Company A is embarking on a three-year project to build and equip a new manufacturing plant and borrows funds to finance the cost. Because of its size and credit status, it has to borrow at variable rates.

It can reasonably estimate what additional returns its new plant will generate but, because the interest it is paying will be variable, it is exposed to the risk that the project may turn out to be uneconomic if interest rates rise unexpectedly.

If the company could secure fixed rate finance, it could remove the risk of interest rate variations and more accurately predict the returns it can make from its investment.

To do this, Company A could enter into an interest rate swap with an investment bank.

As part of the swap, it pays a fixed rate to the investment bank and in exchange receives an amount of interest calculated on a variable rate. With the amount it receives from the investment bank, it then has the funds to settle its variable rate lending.

In this way, it has hedged its interest rate exposure risk.

The two exchanges of cash flow are known as the legs of the swap and the amounts to be exchanged are calculated by reference to a notional amount. The notional amount in the above example would be the amount that Company A has borrowed to fund its project.

Typically, one party will pay an amount based on a fixed rate to the other party, who will pay back an amount of interest that is variable and usually based on LIBOR (London Inter-Bank Offered Rate). The variable rate will usually be set as LIBOR plus, say, 0.5% and will be reset quarterly.

END OF CHAPTER QUESTIONS

Think of an answer for each question and refer to the appropriate section for confirmation.

Question		Answer Reference
1.	What are the four main investment uses of derivatives?	Section 1
2.	What is the key difference between a future and an option?	Sections 2.3 & 3.2
3.	What is the seller of a future known as?	Section 2.4
4.	What is an investor who enters into a contract for the delivery of an asset in three months' time known as?	Section 2.4
5.	What name is given to the seller of an option?	Section 3.3
6.	What type of option gives the holder the right to sell an asset?	Section 3.3
7.	What is the price paid for an option known as and who is it paid to?	Section 3.3
8.	Which type of derivative is not exchange-traded?	Section 4.1
9.	What is an interest rate swap?	Section 4.2

CHAPTER SEVEN

INVESTMENT FUNDS

This syllabus area will provide approximately 8 of the 50 examination questions

The asset management industry forms a major part of the UK's financial services industry and is responsible for the investment management of institutional and retail funds totalling over £3 trillion.

The size and scale of the industry can be seen in the regular reports issued by the Investment Management Association (IMA). The IMA is the trade body for the UK-based asset management industry. Its members manage a wide variety of investment vehicles including authorised investment funds, pension funds and stocks and shares ISAs. Its role is to represent the industry, principally to government and regulators, as well as the press and public and promote high standards.

How its member firms relate to the rest of the industry can be seen from the following diagram.

The UK Investment Market

Source: IMA

Some of the key results from its 7th Asset Management Survey, published in July 2009, are as follows:

- Assets managed in the UK at end December 2008 totalled an estimated £3 trillion.
- 76% of assets managed in the UK are invested on behalf of institutional investors and 24% on behalf of the retail market.
- Over 25,000 people are directly employed in the asset management industry.
- IMA member firms hold approximately 43% of the UK stock market.
- The revenue earned by UK based asset management firms was £9.4 billion.

1. INTRODUCTION

Before we consider the benefits of collective investment and the range of investment styles that are available, we should first look at some of the key considerations that an individual should take into account when determining where to invest and at the type of investment funds that are available.

Before making any investments, an individual should consider some of the following points:

- **What am I investing for?** – the answer, be it retirement, to meet school fees or any other reason, will give some direction to the type of investment that may be suitable.
- **What amount of money will I need?** – an assessment of how much money will eventually be needed determines how much will need to be invested to achieve that goal and whether this is affordable.
- **Over what timescale do I want investment returns?** – this, along with the reason for investing, will give the timescale over which investment needs to be made.
- **What risks am I prepared to take?** – if an individual is going to invest, they will need to be prepared to take some risk in the hope of greater reward. They must be prepared to see at least some fall in the value of their investment without panicking and be willing to hold on in the hope of future gains. If they are not prepared to take any risk whatsoever, then investing in the stock market is not the right option.
- **What types of assets are right for me?** – each type of asset carries risks and these need to be understood so that the right type of asset can be selected that can meet the individual's long term objective with an acceptable level of risk.
- **How can I avoid risk?** – risk cannot be totally avoided but diversifying the range of assets held reduces the risks that are faced.
- **What mix of investments is best suited to my objectives and attitude to risk?** – the right mix of assets – cash, bonds, shares and property – that is best suited will depend on the individual's investment objective, their attitude to risk and the timescale over which they are investing. The mix will also need to change if the individual's circumstances change and as the time when the investment funds are needed approaches.
- **Do I need income now or later?** – if income is taken to spend, then the investment will grow more slowly, whereas if it is reinvested, it will allow interest to be earned on interest and this compounding of interest will generate further growth.

This is only a brief consideration of some of the many questions that all individuals need to consider both before investing and when reviewing existing investments, so individuals are well advised to seek professional advice from a qualified financial adviser.

1.1 Benefits of Collective Investment

LEARNING OBJECTIVES

7.1.1   Understand the benefits of collective investment

Collective investment schemes (funds) pool the resources of a large number of investors, with the aim of pursuing a common investment objective.

This pooling of funds brings a number of benefits, including:

- economies of scale;
- diversification;
- access to professional investment management;
- access to geographical markets, asset classes or investment strategies which might otherwise be inaccessible to the individual investor;

- in many cases, benefit of regulatory oversight; and
- in some cases, tax deferral.

An investor needs a substantial amount of money before he can create a diversified portfolio of investments directly. If an investor has only £3,000 to invest and wants to buy the shares of 30 different companies, each investment would be £100. This would result in a large amount of the £3,000 being spent on commission, since there will be minimum commission rates of, say, £10 on each purchase.

Alternatively, an investment of £3,000 might go into a fund with, say, 80 different investments, but because the investment is being pooled with lots of other investors the commission, as a proportion of the fund, is very small.

The value of shares and most other investments can fall as well as rise. Some might fall spectacularly, for example, shares in a company that suddenly collapses, such as Northern Rock and Lehman Brothers. However, where an investor holds a diversified pool of investments in a portfolio, the risk of single constituent investments falling spectacularly should normally be offset by outperformance on the part of other investments. In other words, risk is lessened when the investor holds a diversified portfolio of investments (of course, the 'risk' of a startling outperformance is also diversified away – but many investors are happy with this if it reduces their risk of total or significant loss).

A fund might also be invested in shares from many different sectors; this achieves diversification from an industry perspective (thereby reducing the risk of investing in a number of shares whose performance is closely correlated). Alternatively it may invest in a variety of bonds or a mix of cash, equities, bonds and property. Some collective investments put limited amounts of investment into bank deposits and even other collective investments.

The other main rationale for investing collectively is to access the investing skills of the fund manager. Fund managers follow their chosen markets closely and will carefully consider what to buy and whether to keep or sell their chosen investments. Few investors have the skill, time or inclination to do this as effectively themselves.

However, fund managers do not manage portfolios for nothing. They might charge investors fees to become involved in their collective investments (entry fees or initial charges), to leave the collective investment (exit charges) and annual management fees. These fees are needed to cover the fund managers' salaries, technology, research, their dealing, settlement and risk management systems and provide a profit.

1.2   Investment Styles

LEARNING OBJECTIVES

7.1.2   Understand the range of investment strategies – active v passive

There are a wide range of funds with many different investment objectives and investment styles. Each of these funds has an investment portfolio managed by a fund manager according to a clearly stated set of objectives. An example of an objective is to invest in the shares of UK companies with above average potential for capital growth and to outperform the FTSE All Share index. Other funds' objectives could be to maximise income or to achieve steady growth in capital and income.

In each case it will also be clear what the fund manager will invest in, ie, shares and/or bonds and/or property and/or cash or money market instruments and if derivatives will be used to hedge currency or other market risks.

It is also important to understand the investment style they adopt. This refers to the fund manager's approach to choosing investments and meeting the fund's objectives. In this section we will look at the differences between active and passive management.

Active management seeks to outperform a predetermined benchmark over a specified time period. It does so by employing fundamental and technical analysis to assist in the forecasting of future events, which may be economic or specific to a company, so as to determine the portfolio's holdings and the timing of purchases and sales.

Two commonly used terms in this context are 'top-down' or 'bottom-up'. Top-down means the manager focuses on economic and industry trends rather than the prospects of particular companies. Bottom-up means that the analysis of a company's net assets, future profitability and cash flow and other company specific indicators, is a priority.

Included in the bottom-up approach are a range of investment styles:

- growth investing, which is picking the shares of companies with opportunities to grow in the long term;
- value investing, which is picking shares of companies that are undervalued relative to their present profits or cash flows;
- momentum investing, which is picking the shares whose value is rising on the basis that this rise will continue;
- contrarian investing is the flip side of momentum investing and means picking shares that are out of favour and may have 'hidden' value.

There is also a significant range of styles used by managers of hedge funds. (Hedge funds are considered later in this chapter.)

Passive management is seen in those collective investment funds that are described as index tracker funds. Index tracking, or indexation, involves constructing a portfolio in such a way that it will track, or mimic, the performance of a recognised equity index.

Indexation is undertaken on the assumption that securities markets are efficiently priced and cannot, therefore, be consistently outperformed. Consequently, no attempt is made to forecast future events or outperform the broader market.

The advantages of employing indexation are that:

- Relatively few active portfolio managers consistently outperform benchmark equity indices.
- Once set up, passive portfolios are generally less expensive to run than active portfolios, given a lower ratio of staff to funds managed and lower portfolio turnover.

The disadvantages of adopting indexation include:

- Performance is affected by the need to manage cash flows, rebalance the portfolio to replicate changes in index-constituent weightings and adjust the portfolio for stocks coming into, and falling out of, the index.
- Most indices assume that dividends from constituent equities are reinvested on the ex-dividend (xd) date whereas a passive fund can only invest dividends when received, usually six weeks after the share has been declared ex-dividend.
- Indexed portfolios may not meet all an investor's objectives.
- Indexed portfolios follow the index down in bear markets.

It should be noted that active and passive investment are not necessarily mutually exclusive and there are investment strategies that incorporate both styles, known as core-satellite management. This strategy looks to index, say, 70% to 80% of the portfolio's value (the 'core'), so as to minimise the risk of underperformance, and then fine tuning this by investing the remainder in a number of specialist actively managed funds or individual securities. This is the 'satellite' element of the fund.

1.3   Range of Funds Available

LEARNING OBJECTIVES

7.2.2   Know the types of funds and how they are classified

There are over 2,000 authorised investment funds available to investors and, unsurprisingly, a method of classifying them is needed in order to allow investors to compare funds with similar objectives.

The Investment Management Association (IMA) is the trade body for the UK authorised open-ended funds industry; it maintains a system for classifying funds. The Association of Investment Companies (AIC) occupies a similar role for investment trusts (close-ended companies).

The IMA's classification system contains thirty sectors grouping similar funds together. Most sectors are broadly categorised between those designed to provide 'income' and those designed to provide 'growth'. Those funds that do not fall easily under these two headings are in a third category entitled 'Specialist Funds'.

Each of the sectors is made up of funds investing in similar asset categories, in the same stock market sectors or in the same geographical region. So, for example, under the heading of funds principally targeting income you will find sectors that include UK gilts, UK corporate bonds and global bonds.

The sectors are aimed at the needs of the investor who has a desire to compare funds on a like-for-like basis. Sector classification provides groups of similar funds whose performance can be fairly compared by an investor and their adviser.

1.4   Regulation of Funds

As you would expect, the investment industry has many regulations that are designed to protect investors.

Some of these regulations govern where and how a fund manager can invest and the documentation an investor can expect to receive.

The regulatory regime for UK authorised funds is heavily influenced by EU directives which have been issued in order to promote a single market in investment funds. In the UK, these are implemented by the FSA through its Collective Investment Schemes Sourcebook (COLL).

1.4.1   Authorised versus Unauthorised Funds

LEARNING OBJECTIVES

7.1.3   Know the differences between authorised and unauthorised funds

In the UK, some collective investment schemes are authorised, while others are unauthorised or unregulated funds.

Authorisation is granted by the FSA. Broadly, the FSA will authorise only those schemes that are sufficiently diversified and that invest in a range of permitted assets.

Collective investment schemes that have been authorised by the FSA can be freely marketed in the UK.

Collective investment schemes that have not been authorised by the FSA cannot be marketed to the general public. These unauthorised schemes are perfectly legal, but their marketing must be carried out subject to certain rules and, in some cases, only to certain types of investor.

1.4.2 UCITS

7.1.4   Know the purpose and principal features of UCITS

UCITS stands for 'Undertakings for Collective Investment in Transferable Securities' and refers to a series of EU regulations that were originally designed to facilitate the promotion of funds to retail investors across Europe. A UCITS, therefore, complies with the requirements of these directives, no matter which EU country it is established in.

The directives have been issued with the intention of creating a framework for cross-border sales of investment funds throughout the European Union (EU). They allow an investment fund to be sold throughout the EU, subject to regulation by its home country regulator.

The original directive was issued in 1985 and established a set of EU-wide rules governing collective investment schemes. Funds set up in accordance with these rules could then be sold across the EU, subject to local tax and marketing laws.

Since then, two further directives have been issued which broadened the range of assets a fund can invest in, in particular allowing managers to use derivatives more freely and introduced a common marketing document, the simplified prospectus.

While UCITS regulations are not directly applicable outside the EU, other jurisdictions, such as Switzerland and Hong Kong, recognise UCITS when funds are applying for registration to sell into those countries.

1.4.3   Onshore versus Offshore Funds

7.1.5   Know the differences between onshore and offshore funds

Some UK collective investment schemes are established and operated in the UK and are described as being onshore funds, to contrast them with funds that are established and operated in other jurisdictions.

Collective investment schemes that are established outside the UK are commonly described as offshore funds. They include schemes that are established in the Isle of Man, Luxembourg, Jersey or Guernsey.

Some (but not all) offshore vehicles are less heavily regulated than their UK equivalents, perhaps enabling funds to pursue a more risky strategy.

In addition, offshore funds are likely to be subject to different tax treatment to their onshore equivalents. While some are regarded as more tax-efficient, others are not. For example, a UK investor investing in an offshore fund which does not have **'reporting status'** (a status accorded to certain offshore funds by the UK HM Revenue & Customs)* could suffer punitive taxes on any gains he realised on sale of the fund.

Offshore funds that seek to market into the UK may do so if the FSA is satisfied they meet the FSA's criteria for authorised funds, in which case they are known as 'recognised schemes'.

*(**Note:** In 2009 the UK replaced distributor status with **'reporting status'**, which means funds need not actually distribute all their income, providing that they fully report it.)

2.   UNIT TRUSTS

LEARNING OBJECTIVES

7.2.1   Know the definition of a unit trust

7.2.3   Know the roles of the manager and the trustee

A unit trust is a collective investment scheme in the form of a trust in which the trustee is the legal owner of the underlying assets and the unit holders are the beneficial owners. It may be authorised or unauthorised.

Investors pay money into the trust in exchange for units. The money is invested in a diversified portfolio of assets, usually consisting of shares or bonds or a mix of the two. If the diversified portfolio increases in value, the value of the units will increase. Of course, there is a possibility that the portfolio might fall in value, in which case the units will also decrease in value.

The unit trust is often described as an open-ended collective investment scheme because the trust can grow as more investors buy into the fund, or shrink as investors sell units back to the fund, and they are either cancelled or reissued to new investors.

The role of the unit trust manager is to decide, within the rules of the trust and the various regulations, which investments are included within the unit trust to meet its investment objectives. This will include deciding what to buy and when to buy it, as well as what to sell and when to sell it. The unit trust manager may (and commonly does) outsource this decision-making to a separate investment manager.

The manager also provides a market for the units, by dealing with investors who want to buy or sell units. It also carries out the daily pricing of units, which is based on the Net Asset Value (NAV) of the underlying constituents.

Every unit trust must also appoint a trustee. The trustee is the legal owner of the assets in the trust, holding the assets for the benefit of the underlying unit holders. The trustee also protects the interests of the investors by, among other things, monitoring the actions of the unit trust manager. Whenever new units are created for the trust, they are created by the trustee. The trustees are organisations that the unit holders can trust with their assets; for authorised unit trusts, the trustees are companies subject to special regulation – all part of global banking groups.

3. OPEN-ENDED INVESTMENT COMPANIES (OEICs)

LEARNING OBJECTIVES

7.3.1   Know the definition and legal structure of an OEIC

7.3.2   Know the roles of the authorised corporate director and the depositary

7.3.3   Know the terms ICVC, SICAV and the context in which they are used

An Open-Ended Investment Company (OEIC) is another form of authorised collective investment scheme. OEICs are referred to as Investment Companies with Variable Capital (ICVCs) by the FSA.

An OEIC is a collective investment scheme structured as a company, with the investors holding shares. The OEIC invests shareholders' money in a diversified pool of investments and has the ability to issue more shares or redeem shares as demanded by investors.

As their name suggests, OEICs are companies, but they differ from conventional companies because they are established under special legislation and not the Companies Acts. They must create new shares and redeem existing ones according to investor demand, unlike ordinary companies. This means they are open-ended in nature, as is the case with unit trusts.

When an OEIC is set up, it is a requirement that an Authorised Corporate Director (ACD) and a depositary are appointed.

The ACD is responsible for the day-to-day management of the fund, including managing the investments, valuing and pricing the fund and dealing with investors. It may undertake these activities itself or delegate them to specialist third parties. It is subject to the same requirements as the manager of an authorised unit trust.

The OEIC's investments are held by an independent depositary, responsible for looking after the investments on behalf of the OEIC shareholders and overseeing the activities of the ACD. The depositary occupies a similar role to that of the trustee of an authorised unit trust and is subject to the same regulatory requirements.

The OEIC is the legal owner of the investments and shareholders are the beneficial owners of the value of the company. The register of shareholders is maintained by the ACD.

An ICVC commonly found in Western Europe is the SICAV, which is an acronym for 'Société d'Investissement à Capital Variable'; like a UK OEIC, it is investment company with variable capital. SICAVs are typically set up in Luxembourg by asset management firms so that they can be distributed to investors across Europe or even further.

4.   PRICING, DEALING AND SETTLEMENT

LEARNING OBJECTIVES

7.4.1   Know how unit trusts and OEIC shares are priced

7.4.2   Know the ways in which charges can be made by the fund manager

4.1   Pricing and Charges

The prices at which authorised unit trusts or OEICs are bought and sold are based on the value of the fund's underlying investments.

The authorised fund manager is, however, given the flexibility to quote prices which can be either single-priced or dual-priced (although this decision must be taken at the outset and the manager cannot switch between the two as and when it suits).

Single-pricing refers to the use of the mid-market prices of the underlying assets to produce a single price, while dual-pricing involves using the market's bid and offer prices of the underlying assets to produce separate prices for buying and selling of shares/units in the fund.

Traditionally, authorised unit trusts have used dual-pricing and OEICs have used single-pricing. All funds now have a choice of which pricing methodology they use; whichever is chosen must be disclosed in the prospectus.

Where a fund is single-priced, its underlying investments will be valued based on their mid-market value. This method of pricing does not provide the ability to recoup dealing expenses and commissions within the spread. Such charges can be recouped either by applying a separate charge, known as a 'dilution levy', on purchases or redemptions or by 'swinging' the daily price to a dual priced basis depending on the ratio of buyers and sellers on any day. It is important to note that the initial charge will be charged separately, whichever pricing method is used.

The maximum price at which the fund manager is able to sell new units is prescribed by the FSA. It is known as the maximum buying price and, under dual-pricing, comprises the creation price (ie, the price the manager must pay to the trustee to create new units, which broadly consists of the value of the underlying investments and an allowance for dealing costs) plus the fund manager's initial charge.

EXAMPLE

Value of the portfolio (at offer prices) divided by the number of units	100.00p
Add, allowance for dealing costs: brokerage at, say, ¼%	0.25p
Stamp duty at ½%	0.50p
Subtotal (= creation price)	100.75p
Add, fund manager's initial charge at, say, 6.55%	6.55p
Maximum buying price	107.30p

The actual buying price does not have to be 107.30p and, because of the sensitivity of investors to charges, the fund manager may feel that a lower price of, say, 103p per unit is more appropriate.

The price at which the fund manager will repurchase units is calculated in a similar manner. From the investor's viewpoint it is referred to as the selling price and the minimum selling price is also the cancellation price, ie, the price received from the fund by the manager when he cancels the units, using as its starting point the value of the portfolio at bid prices. Again, the manager has flexibility about the price that is set subject to it being no less than the minimum selling price.

The prices of most individual funds are provided in broadsheet newspapers each day. The telephone numbers and addresses of the fund managers are normally provided alongside the prices.

4.2 Dealing and Settlement

LEARNING OBJECTIVES

7.4.3   Know how shares and units are bought and sold

7.4.4   Know how collectives are settled

Investors can buy or sell units in a number of ways:

- direct with the fund manager (either by telephone, via the internet or by post); or
- via their broker or financial adviser; or
- through a fund supermarket.

A fund supermarket is an organisation that specialises in offering investors easy access to a range of unit trusts and OEICs from different providers. They are usually based around an internet platform which takes the investor's order and processes it on their behalf, usually at reduced commission rates. Fund supermarkets offer online dealing, valuations, portfolio planning tools and access to key features documents and illustrations. Investors can look at their various holdings in different funds in one place, analyse their performance and easily make switches from one fund to another.

Whether an investor wishes to buy or sell his units, they will be either bought from, or sold back to, the authorised fund manager. There is no active secondary market in units or shares, except between the investors (or their advisers/intermediaries) and the fund manager.

The key point to note, therefore, is that units in authorised unit trusts and shares in OEICs are bought from the managers themselves and not via a stock market.

Where an order to buy or sell units is undertaken by an organisation that provides dealing services, such as a fund supermarket, it is likely to use a systems platform to place those orders with the fund management group.

One widely used system is EMX, which can be used by firms to enter customer orders, aggregate these and then send them electronically to the fund group. The firm then receives an electronic confirmation of receipt and, once the deal is traded at the next valuation point, EMX will send an electronic dealing confirmation showing the price at which the deal was done.

EMX was taken over by Euroclear, the parent company that owns CREST, in late 2006 and it has announced plans to use this to build an automated, straight-through processing platform for fund dealing and settlement.

Settlement currently takes place directly with each fund group. For purchases, once the investment has been made and the amount invested has been received, the fund group will record ownership of the relevant number of units or shares in the fund's share register. When the investor decides to sell he/she need to instruct the fund manager (or ask his/her adviser or the supermarket to instruct the fund manager) who then has four days, from receipt of the instruction, in which to settle the sale and remit the proceeds to the investor. Traditionally, this instruction had to be in writing, but from 2009 managers, supermarkets or advisers are able to accept instruction via the internet or over the telephone, using appropriate security checks.

5.   INVESTMENT TRUSTS

LEARNING OBJECTIVES

7.5.1   Know the characteristics of an investment trust: share classes; gearing

7.5.2   Understand the factors that affect the price of an investment trust

7.5.3   Know the meaning of the discounts and premiums in relation to investment trusts

7.5.4   Know how investment trust shares are traded

Despite its name, an investment trust is actually a company, not a trust. It is a listed company and has directors and shareholders. However, like a unit trust, an investment trust will invest in a diversified range of investments, allowing its shareholders to diversify and lessen their risk.

When a new investment trust is established and launched, it issues shares to new investors. Unlike an authorised unit trust or OEIC, the number of shares is likely to remain fixed for many years. As a result, investment trusts are closed-ended, in contrast with authorised unit trusts and OEICs which are open-ended.

The cash from the new issue of shares will be invested in a number of other investments, mainly the shares of other companies. If the value of the investments grows then the value of the investment trust company's shares should rise too.

Some investment trust companies have more than one type of share. For example, an investment trust might issue both ordinary shares and preference shares. Preference shares may be issued on different terms and may, for example, be issued as convertible preference shares that are convertible into the ordinary shares or as zero dividend preference (ZDP) shares. As the name suggests, ZDPs receive no dividends and the investor instead receives their return on the difference in the price they paid and the amount they receive when the ZDP is repaid at a fixed future date.

In contrast with OEICs and authorised unit trusts, investment trust companies are allowed to borrow more money on a long-term basis by taking out bank loans and/or issuing bonds. This can enable them to invest the borrowed money in more stocks and shares – a process known as 'gearing'. This approach can improve returns when markets are rising, but when markets are falling it can exacerbate losses. As a result, the greater the level of gearing used by an investment trust the greater will be the risk.

The price of a share (except in the case of an OEIC, as we have seen) is what someone is prepared to pay for it. The price of an investment trust company (ITC) share is no different.

The share price of an ITC is thus arrived at in a very different way to the unit price of an authorised unit trust or the share price of an OEIC.

Remember that units in an authorised unit trust are bought and sold by its fund manager at a price that is based on the underlying value of the constituent investments. Similarly, shares in an OEIC are bought and sold by the ACD, again at the value of the underlying investments.

The share price of an investment trust company, however, is not necessarily the same as the value of the underlying investments. The value of the underlying investments determined on a per share basis is referred to as the net asset value and, because the share price is driven by supply and demand factors, it may be above or below the net asset value.

When the investment trust share price is above the net asset value, it is said to be trading at a premium. When the investment trust share price is below the net asset value, it is said to be trading at a discount.

EXAMPLE

ABC Investment Trust shares are trading at £2.30. The net asset value per share is £2.00. ABC Investment Trust shares are trading at a premium. The premium is 15% of the underlying net asset value.

EXAMPLE

XYZ Investment Trust shares are trading at 95p. The net asset value per share is £1.00. XYZ Investment Trust shares are trading at a discount. The discount is 5% of the underlying net asset value.

Investment trust company shares generally trade at a discount to their net asset value and the extent of the discount is calculated daily and shown in the business pages of newspapers.

A number of factors contribute to the extent of the discount and it will vary across different investment trust companies. Most importantly, the discount is a function of the market's view of the quality of the investment trust, and its choice of underlying investments. A smaller discount (or even a premium) will be displayed where investment trusts are nearing their winding-up, or about to undergo some corporate activity such as a merger/takeover. (You should note that some, but not all, investment trusts have a predetermined date at which the trust will be wound up and the assets returned to the shareholders.)

In the same way as other listed company shares, shares in investment trust companies are bought and sold on the London Stock Exchange using the SETS trading system.

HOTSPOT

7

Go online to your elearning product for further information on investment trusts.

If you haven't purchased your elearning product, you can order now by calling Client Services on +44(0)20 7645 0680.

---

6.   REAL ESTATE INVESTMENT TRUSTS (REITs)

LEARNING OBJECTIVES

7.6.1   Know the basics characteristics of REITs: tax efficient; property diversification; liquidity; risk

---

REITs are normal investment trust companies that pool investors' funds to invest in commercial and, possibly, residential property. They became available to UK investors from January 2007 and the main quoted property companies, such as Land Securities and British Land, have converted to REIT status.

One of the main features of REITs is that they provide access to property returns without the previous disadvantage of double taxation. Prior to the introduction of REITs, where an investor held property company shares, not only would the company pay corporation tax, but the investor would be liable to income tax on any dividends and capital gains tax on any growth. Under the rules, the REIT pays no tax on property income or capital gains on property disposals, providing that at least 90% of that income (after expenses) is distributed to shareholders. These property income distributions are then taxed in the hands of the investor as if he/she had received that income directly himself/herself (ie, it is not taxed as a dividend).

REITs may also be held in both Individual Savings Accounts (ISAs) and Self-Invested Personal Pension Schemes (SIPPS).

REITs give investors access to professional property investment and provide new opportunities, such as the ability to invest in commercial property. This allows investors to diversify the risk of holding direct property investments.

This type of investment trust company will also remove a further risk from holding direct property, namely liquidity risk or the risk that the investment will not be able to be readily realised. REITs are quoted on the London Stock Exchange and other trading venues like other investment trusts and dealt in the same way.

7. EXCHANGE-TRADED FUNDS (ETFs)

LEARNING OBJECTIVES

7.7.1   Know the main characteristics of exchange-traded funds

7.7.2   Know how exchange-traded funds are traded

An Exchange-Traded Fund (ETF) is an investment fund, usually designed to track a particular index.

This is typically a stock market index, such as the FTSE 100. The investor buys shares in the ETF which are quoted on the stock exchange, like investment trusts. However, unlike investment trusts, ETFs are 'open-ended funds'. This means that, like OEICs, the fund gets bigger as more people invest and gets smaller as people withdraw their money.

ETF shares may trade at a premium or discount to the underlying investments, but the difference is minimal and the ETF share price essentially reflects the value of the investments in the fund. The investor's return is in the form of dividends paid by the ETF and the possibility of a capital gain (or loss) on sale.

In London, ETFs are traded on the London Stock Exchange, which has established a special subset of the Exchange for ETFs, called extraMARK. Shares in ETFs are bought and sold via stockbrokers and exhibit the following charges:

- There is a spread between the price at which investors buy the shares and the price at which they can sell them. This is usually very small, for example, just 0.1 or 0.2% for, say, an ETF tracking the FTSE 100.
- An annual management charge is deducted from the fund. Typically, this is 0.5% or less.
- The investors pay stockbroker's commission when they buy and sell. However, unlike other shares, there is no stamp duty to pay on purchases.

Comparison between Investment Companies

The following table summarises the main points about each type of collective investment scheme.

	Authorised Unit Trusts	**OEICs**	**Investment Trusts**	**Exchange-Traded Funds**
Legal Structure	Trust	Company	Company	Company
Management	Authorised Manager (company)	Authorised Corporate Director (company)	Board of Directors	Management Company
Supervision	Trustee	Depositary	Board of Directors	Depositary
Regulation	FSA	FSA	UK Listing Authority	FSA and UK Listing Authority
Open or closed-ended	Open	Open	Closed	Open
Pricing	Single- or dual-priced	Single- or dual-priced	Dependent on demand and supply	Based on net asset value
Trading	Authorised Manager	Authorised Corporate Director	Stock Market	Stock Market
Settlement	Authorised Manager	Authorised Corporate Director	CREST	CREST

8. HEDGE FUNDS

LEARNING OBJECTIVES

7.8.1   Know the basic characteristics of hedge funds: risk and risk types; cost and liquidity; investment strategies

Hedge funds are reputed to be high risk. However, in some cases, this perception stands at odds with reality. In their original incarnation, hedge funds sought to eliminate or reduce market risk. That said, there are now many different styles of hedge fund – some risk-averse, and some employing highly risky strategies. It is, therefore, not wise to generalise about them.

The most obvious market risk is the risk that is faced by an investor in shares – as the broad market moves down, the investor's shares also fall in value.

Traditional 'absolute return' hedge funds attempt to profit regardless of the general movements of the market, by carefully selecting a combination of asset classes, including derivatives and by holding both long and short positions (a short position may involve the selling of shares which the investor does not at that time own in the hope of buying them back more cheaply if the market falls. Alternatively, it may involve the use of derivatives, as we have already seen).

However, innovation has resulted in a wide range of complex hedge fund strategies, some of which place a greater emphasis on producing highly geared returns than controlling market risk.

Many hedge funds have high initial investment levels meaning that access is effectively restricted to wealthy investors and institutions. However, investors can also gain access to hedge funds through funds of hedge funds.

The common aspects of hedge funds are the following:

- **Structure** – most hedge funds are established as unauthorised and, therefore, unregulated, collective investment schemes, meaning that they cannot be generally marketed to private individuals because they are considered too risky for the less financially sophisticated investor.
- **High investment entry levels** – most hedge funds require minimum investments in excess of £50,000; some exceed £1 million.
- **Investment flexibility** – because of the lack of regulation, hedge funds are able to invest in whatever assets they wish (subject to compliance with the restrictions in their constitutional documents and prospectus). In addition to being able to take long and short positions in securities like shares and bonds, some take positions in commodities and currencies. Their investment style is generally aimed at producing 'absolute' returns – positive returns regardless of the general direction of market movements.
- **Gearing** – many hedge funds can borrow funds and use derivatives to potentially enhance their returns.
- **Prime broker** – hedge funds buy and sell investments from, borrow from and, often, entrust the safekeeping of their assets to one main wholesale broker called their prime broker.
- **Liquidity** – to maximise the hedge fund manager's investment freedom, hedge funds usually impose an initial 'lock-in' period of between one and three months before investors can sell on their investments.
- **Cost** – hedge funds typically levy performance-related fees, which the investor pays if certain performance levels are achieved, otherwise paying a fee comparable to that charged by other growth funds. Performance fees can be substantial, with 20% or more of the 'net new highs' being common.

END OF CHAPTER QUESTIONS

Think of an answer for each question and refer to the appropriate section for confirmation.

Question	Answer Reference
1. How might pooling of investment aid a retail investor?	Section 1.1
2. What is an investment management approach that seeks to produce returns in line with an index known as?	Section 1.2
3. Why would an investment fund seek UCITS status?	Section 1.4.2
4. Who is the legal owner of the investments held in an OEIC?	Section 3
5. In which type of collective investment vehicle would you most likely expect to see a fund manager quote bid and offer prices?	Section 4.1
6. How does the trading and settlement of an authorised unit trust differ from an ETF?	Section 4.2
7. What are some of the principal ways in which investment trusts differ from authorised unit trusts and OEICS?	Section 5
8. What percentage of property income (net of expenses) needs to be distributed to qualify for REIT status?	Section 6
9. Which is an open-ended type of investment vehicle that is traded on a stock exchange?	Section 7
10. What type of investment vehicle makes extensive use of short positions?	Section 8

CHAPTER EIGHT

FINANCIAL SERVICES REGULATION

This syllabus area will provide approximately 6 of the 50 examination questions

An understanding of regulation is essential in today's investment world and in this chapter we will consider some of the key aspects of UK regulation.

1.   FINANCIAL SERVICES AND MARKETS ACT

LEARNING OBJECTIVES

8.1.1   Know the function of the following in the financial services industry: regulators (FSA/E commission/committee of European securities regulators)

As this section considers UK regulation, much of the material has been sourced from publications made by the Financial Services Authority (FSA), the UK regulator.

1.1   Role of Regulators

As well as aiming to ensure that the EU has world class regulatory standards, the EU is also particularly concerned with the development of a single market in financial services across Europe.

This has been a major feature of European financial services legislation for some time and is the cornerstone of the Financial Services Action Plan (FSAP).

In the following sections we will look at how the EU introduces new regulation and how this gets translated into new rules in each EU country.

EU regulation comes about by way of a tiered approach to its creation and implementation.

Commonly, the approach used is known as the 'Lamfalussy Process', named after the chairman of the advisory committee who devised it. It is comprised of four levels:

- The first level involves the European Council and the European Parliament adopting in a co-decision procedure a piece of legislation, a framework directive, which establishes the core elements of regulation and sets guidelines for its implementation.
- The laws then progress to the second level, where sector-specific committees and regulators advise on the technical detail. The European Commission, based on this advice, then issues binding (only binding if a regulation – directives have to be implemented nationally) rules at a detailed level which do not have to go through the often lengthy co-decision process.
- At the third level, national regulators work on co-ordinating new regulations with other nations.
- The fourth level involves compliance and enforcement of the new rules and laws at national level by the European Commission.

On legislation related to securities markets the Commission is guided in its implementation by the Committee of European Securities Regulators (CESR), which co-ordinates regulatory input from European securities regulators into the level two advice. On level three CESR works to develop non-binding guidance for its members to ensure common and uniform implementation of EU rules.

This process was used to introduce the Markets in Financial Instruments Directive (MiFID).

1.2   FSMA 2000

8.1.2   Understand the need for regulation and the purpose of the financial services and markets act 2000

The financial services sector underwent a radical change on 1 December 2001 when the Financial Services and Markets Act of 2000 (FSMA 2000) came into force. Before FSMA 2000, the various sectors of the industry were covered by a series of laws and the requirements of a mix of statutory and self-regulating organisations, regarded by some as unnecessarily complex and confusing.

Under FSMA 2000, the government delegated overall responsibility for the regulation of the financial services industry to the FSA.

1.3   Financial Services Authority (FSA)

8.1.3   Know the four statutory objectives of the financial services authority

FSMA 2000 sets out what is expected from the FSA by giving it four statutory objectives. The objectives are to:

*   maintain confidence in the UK financial system;
*   reduce the scope for financial crime;
*   promote the public's awareness of the financial system; and
*   ensure the appropriate degree of protection for consumers.

HM Treasury is responsible for oversight of how the FSA conducts its operations and so the FSA is accountable to Treasury Ministers, and through them to Parliament.

1.4   Authorisation

8.1.4   Understand the reasons for authorisation of firms and approved persons

FSMA 2000 makes it an offence for a firm to provide financial services in the UK without being authorised to do so. There are certain exemptions from this requirement, for example, for the Bank of England.

Authorisation is granted by the FSA, which looks at each applicant to assess whether the firm is 'fit and proper' and meets the threshold conditions. Before granting authorisation, the FSA considers the company's management, financial strength and the calibre of its staff. The latter is particularly important in certain key roles, which the FSA refers to as 'controlled functions'.

By only allowing 'fit and proper' firms to be involved in the financial services industry, the FSA begins to satisfy its statutory objectives of maintaining confidence in the financial system and of providing appropriate investor protection.

Authorised persons are firms but, as firms, they are ultimately operated by individuals – the directors and employees.

When a firm applies for authorisation (and when there are changes to key staffing roles) the FSA will assess the calibre of these individuals. Particular individuals, fulfilling key roles within the firm, known as 'controlled functions', have to be approved by the FSA.

These individuals are approved only if they are fit and proper. The fit and proper assessment looks for three things:

* Honesty, integrity and reputation. Here the FSA will consider such issues as any criminal record or history of regulatory misconduct.
* Competence and capability to fulfil the role, including achieving success in certain regulatory examinations.
* Financial soundness. Here the FSA will consider the capital adequacy of the applicant and his/her financial history, for instance an undischarged bankrupt would be unlikely to be approved for many roles.

1.5   Controlled Functions

LEARNING OBJECTIVES

8.1.6   Know the five groups of activity (controlled functions) requiring approved person status

Controlled functions are those involved in dealing with customers or their investments, key managers in the firm including finance, compliance and risk and those exercising a measure of control over the firm as a whole.

The FSA classifies controlled functions into five groups, four of which are 'significant influence functions':

* **Governing functions** – for example, the directors of the firm.
* **Significant management function** – senior managers in the larger firms, like the head of equity dealing.
* **Systems and control function** – mainly those responsible for risk management and internal audit.
* **Required functions** – specific roles, such as the director or senior manager responsible for compliance oversight.

The fifth group comprises:

- **Customer function** – for example, those individuals managing investments or providing advice to customers.

1.6   Principles-Based Regulation and Treating Customers Fairly

8.1.5   Understand the purpose of the FSA's principles-based approach to regulation

8.1.7   Know the FSA's six outcomes for treating customers fairly

There are two broad approaches to financial regulation:

- One approach is based on specific legal rules which must be obeyed. This is known as the 'statutory approach' and is practised, for example, in the US by the Securities and Exchange Commission (SEC) which regulates non-banking financial activity.
- The other approach is to set out in more general terms the types of behaviour that are expected of firms and individuals. This is known as the 'principles-based approach' and is practised in the UK by the FSA.

Neither approach is perfect, but adherents of principles-based regulation favour it because they believe that it is impossible to write a rule for every specific situation that a regulated firm might encounter.

On the other hand, many practitioners operating in compliance or legal departments are more comfortable with a rules-based approach. When operating under a principles-based regime, they tend to seek detailed guidance on how to interpret principles in specific situations.

Principles-based regulation involves setting broad principles to which firms should adhere, but which essentially leaves it up to firms to determine how they are implemented. In this way, FSA believes that a compliant culture can be better built up and one that can adapt to the rapid pace of change in the industry.

Principles-based regulation, however, means placing greater reliance on outcomes. The FSA has as part of its reaction to the market failures of 2008 announced its intention to deliver more intensive supervision and credible deterrence and as part of this, emphasised the importance it will attach to the achievement of these regulatory outcomes.

The Treating Customers Fairly initiative is a major part of this approach.

The FSA retail agenda focuses on delivering an effective and efficient retail market for financial services and products and through this a fair deal for consumers. FSA publications state that this requires:

- capable and confident consumers;
- clear, simple and understandable information provided for, and used by, consumers;
- soundly managed and well-capitalised firms which treat their customers fairly; and
- regulation that is proportionate and risk-based.

One of its key priorities for delivering this agenda is the Treating Customers Fairly initiative.

The requirement for firms to treat their customers fairly is firmly rooted in the Principles for Businesses. Principle 6 states that 'a firm must pay due regard to the interests of its customers and treat them fairly'. This is, therefore, not a new obligation but the FSA is giving it renewed emphasis to encourage firms to consider for themselves how they deliver fair treatment to their customers.

The approach the FSA has adopted to Treating Customers Fairly has been not to define precisely what constitutes 'treating customers fairly', but rather to challenge the senior management of firms to work this out for themselves, taking into account the particular types of business that they undertake. Its objective is for this to be embedded into the culture of a firm at all levels, so that over time it becomes 'business as usual'.

As a result, it requires firms to go beyond simply meeting a detailed set of rules and instead to consider the outcome of the services they provide to their clients. The FSA has defined six 'consumer outcomes' to explain what firms should be aiming to achieve. These are:

- Consumers can be confident that they are dealing with firms where the fair treatment of customers is central to the corporate culture.
- Products and services marketed and sold in the retail market are designed to meet the needs of identified consumer groups and are targeted accordingly.
- Consumers are provided with clear information and are kept appropriately informed before, during and after the point of sale.
- Where consumers receive advice, the advice is suitable and takes account of their circumstances.
- Consumers are provided with products that perform as firms have led them to expect and the associated service is both of an acceptable standard and as they have been led to expect.
- Consumers do not face unreasonable post-sale barriers imposed by firms to change products, switch provider, submit a claim or make a complaint.

The FSA will look for evidence that firms really have incorporated Treating Customers Fairly throughout their operations and processes. It expects to see this incorporated into a firm's systems and controls and all aspects of the business culture, including people issues such as training and competence, remuneration and performance management.

It also expects senior management to ensure that they have the right management information and other data to enable them to satisfy themselves that they are treating their customers fairly in practice.

1.7   Financial Services and Markets Tribunal

LEARNING OBJECTIVES

8.1.8   Know the role of the financial services and markets tribunal

As a result of its powers, the FSA is able to impose decisions or sanctions on firms and individuals, including disciplinary decisions and financial penalties. There is a risk that it might make mistakes in these decisions. An appeal process has been established to ensure compliance with human rights legislation when disagreements arise over the FSA's regulatory decisions which need to be resolved.

When this occurs, the matter can be referred to the Financial Services and Markets Tribunal, which is run by the Ministry of Justice (formerly the Department of Constitutional Affairs). The tribunal is a judicial body created under FSMA 2000 and is composed of eight legally qualified chairmen and 19 lay members. Those that wish to contest FSA decisions refer cases to the tribunal which considers what action should be taken and then issues binding directions to the FSA.

2.   MONEY LAUNDERING

LEARNING OBJECTIVES

8.2.1   Know what money laundering is and the related criminal offences

8.2.2   Know the purpose and the main provisions of the proceeds of crime act 2002 and the money laundering regulations 2007

8.2.3   Understand the three main stages of money laundering

8.2.4   Know the action to be taken by those employed in financial services if money laundering activity is suspected

8.2.5   Know what constitutes satisfactory evidence of identity

Money laundering is the process of turning money that is derived from criminal activities, **'dirty money'**, into money which appears to have been legitimately acquired and which can therefore be more easily invested and spent.

Money laundering can take many forms including:

- turning money acquired through criminal activity into **'clean money'**;
- handling the proceeds of crimes such as theft, fraud and tax evasion;
- handling stolen goods;
- being directly involved with or facilitating the laundering of any criminal or terrorist property;
- criminals investing the proceeds of their crimes in the whole range of financial products.

There can be considerable similarities between the movement of terrorist funds and the laundering of criminal property. Because terrorist groups can have links with other criminal activities there is inevitably some overlap between anti-money laundering provisions and the rules designed to prevent the financing of terrorist acts.

However, these are two major differences to note between terrorist financing and other money laundering activities:

- Often, only quite small sums of money are required to commit terrorist acts, making identification and tracking more difficult.
- If legitimate funds are used to fund terrorist activities, it is difficult to identify when the funds become 'terrorist funds'.

Terrorist organisations can, however, require significant funding and will employ modern techniques to manage them and transfer the funds between jurisdictions, hence the similarities with money laundering.

There are three stages to a successful money laundering operation:

- **Placement** – is the first stage and typically involves placing the criminally derived cash into some form of bank or building society account.
- **Layering** – is the second stage and involves moving the money around in order to make it difficult for the authorities to link the placed funds with the ultimate beneficiary of the money. Disguising the original source of the funds might involve buying and selling foreign currencies, shares or bonds.
- **Integration** – is the third and final stage. At this stage, the layering has been successful and the ultimate beneficiary appears to be holding legitimate funds ('clean' money rather than 'dirty' money). The money is integrated back into the financial system and dealt with as if it were legitimate.

2.1   Legal and Regulatory Framework

LEARNING OBJECTIVES

8.2.2   Know the purpose and the main provisions of the Proceeds of Crime Act 2002 and the Money Laundering Regulations 2007

The cross-border nature of money laundering and terrorist financing has lead to international co-ordination to ensure that countries have legislation and regulatory processes in place to enable identification and prosecution of those involved.

Examples include:

- The Financial Action Task Force has issued recommendations aimed at setting minimum standards for action in different countries to ensure that anti-money laundering efforts are consistent internationally and has also issued special recommendations on terrorist financing.
- EU directives targeted at money laundering prevention.
- Standards issued by international bodies to encourage due diligence procedures to be followed for customer identification.

- Sanctions by the UN and the EU to deny individuals and organisations from certain countries access to the financial services sector.
- Guidance issued by the private sector Wolfsberg Group of banks in relation to private banking, correspondent banking and other activities.

In the UK, the approach has been to specify the key elements of the anti-money laundering and countering terrorist financing regime (AML/CTF) as objectives, leaving UK financial firms the discretion as to how these should be implemented, using a risk-based approach.

The main laws and regulations relating to money laundering and terrorist financing are:

- Proceeds of Crime Act 2002;
- Terrorism Act 2000, as amended by the Anti-Terrorism, Crime and Security Act 2001;
- Money Laundering Regulations 2007;
- HM Treasury Sanctions Notices and news releases;
- FSA Handbook; and
- JMLSG guidance.

The Proceeds of Crime Act 2002 (as amended) consolidated and extended existing UK legislation regarding money laundering and established three broad groups of offences related to money laundering that firms and the staff working for them need to avoid committing:

- knowingly assisting in concealing, or arranging for the acquisition, use or possession of criminal property;
- failing to report knowledge or suspicions of possible money laundering;
- tipping off another person that a money laundering report has been made that might prejudice the investigation.

It also made it an offence to impede any investigation including:
- destroying or disposing of any documents that are relevant to an investigation;
- failure by a firm to comply with a customer information order.

The maximum prison terms that can be imposed under the Act are 14 years for the offence of money laundering and five years for failing to make a report, tipping off or destroying relevant documents. In each case, the penalties can be imprisonment and/or an unlimited fine.

The Terrorism Act establishes a series of offences related to involvement in arrangements for facilitating, raising or using funds for terrorism purposes. As with money laundering, there is a duty to report suspicions and it is an offence to fail to report where there are reasonable grounds to have a suspicion or to be involved in an arrangement that facilitates the retention or control of terrorist property by concealment, removal from the jurisdiction, transfer to nominees or in any other way. The maximum penalties under the act are five years' imprisonment and/or a fine for failure to report and 14 years and/or a fine for money laundering.

The Money Laundering Regulations 2007 implemented the EU directive on money laundering and specify the arrangement that firms must have in place covering:

- customer due diligence;
- reporting;

- record keeping;
- internal control;
- risk assessment and management;
- compliance management; and
- communication.

HM Treasury maintains a list of individuals and organisations that are subject to financial sanctions and it is a criminal offence to make payments or to allow payments to be made to any of these.

The FSA Handbook requires firms to have effective systems and controls for countering the risk that a firm might be used to further financial crime and has specific provisions regarding money laundering risks.

HOTSPOT **8**	Go online to your elearning product for further information on legal and regulatory framework. If you haven't purchased your elearning product, you can order now by calling Client Services on +44(0)20 7645 0680.

2.2 Action Required by Firms and Individuals

LEARNING OBJECTIVES

8.2.4 Know the action to be taken by those employed in financial services if money laundering activity is suspected

8.2.5 Know what constitutes satisfactory evidence of identity

As mentioned above, it is up to firms how they implement the requirements of the legislation and the regulations.

The Proceeds of Crime Act, the Terrorism Act and the Money Laundering Regulations require a court to take account of industry guidance when considering whether a person or firm has committed an offence or has complied with the money laundering regulations. This guidance is provided by the Joint Money Laundering Steering Group (JMLSG), an industry body made up of 17 financial sector trade bodies.

Its latest guidance sets out what is expected of firms and their staff. It emphasises the responsibility of senior management to manage the firm's money laundering and terrorist financing risks and how this should be carried out on a risk-based approach. It sets out a standard approach to the identification and verification of customers, separating out basic identity from other aspects of customer due diligence measures, as well as giving guidance on the obligation to monitor customer activity.

The following sections highlight some of the principal features of the latest guidance.

2.2.1 Internal Controls

There is a requirement for firms to establish and maintain appropriate and risk-based policies and procedures in order to prevent operations related to money laundering or terrorist financing. These controls are expected to be appropriate to the risks faced by the firm.

2.2.2 Money Laundering Reporting Officer (MLRO)

Firms are expected to appoint a nominated officer, or a Money Laundering Reporting Officer (MLRO), who is responsible for oversight of the firm's compliance with the FSA's rules on systems and controls against money laundering.

The MLRO must receive and review internal disclosure reports and make external reports to the Serious Organised Crime Agency (SOCA) where required. The MLRO is also required to carry out regular assessments of the adequacy of the firm's systems and controls and to produce a report at least annually to senior management on its effectiveness.

The MLRO must have authority to act independently and senior management must ensure that they have sufficient resources available to effectively carry out their responsibilities.

2.2.3 Risk-Based Approach

Senior management are expected to ensure that they have appropriate systems and controls in place to manage the risks associated with the business and its customers.

This requires them to assess their money laundering/terrorist financing risk in some way and decide how they will manage it. It also requires them to determine appropriate customer due diligence measures to be undertaken to ensure customer identification and acceptance procedures reflect the risk characteristics of customers' based on the type of customer and the business relationship, product or transaction.

2.2.4 Customer Due Diligence (CDD)

The Money Laundering Regulations 2007 set out a firm's obligations to conduct customer due diligence and describe customers and products where no, or limited, CDD measures are required and those customers and circumstances where enhanced due diligence is required.

The CDD measures that must be carried out involve:

- identifying the customer and verifying their identity;
- identifying the beneficial owner, where relevant, and verifying their identity;
- obtaining information of the purpose and intended nature of the business relationship.

Firms must also conduct ongoing monitoring of the business relationship with their customers to identify any unusual activity.

For some particular customers, products or transactions Simplified Due Diligence (SDD) may be applied. Firms must have reasonable grounds for believing that it falls within one of the allowed categories and be able to demonstrate this to their supervisory authority. SDD may be applied to:

- certain other regulated firms in the financial sector;
- companies listed on a regulated market;
- beneficial owners of pooled accounts held by notaries or independent legal professionals;
- UK public authorities;
- community institutions;
- certain life assurance and e-money products;
- certain pension funds;
- certain low risk products;
- child trust funds.

In cases of higher risk and if the customer is not physically present when their identities are verified then Enhanced Due Diligence (EDD) measures must be applied on a risk sensitive basis.

The JMLSG Guidance Notes provide extensive guidance on the customer due diligence to be applied and the above should be regarded as a very brief summary only; however, the core obligations on firms can be summarised as follows:

- must carry out prescribed CDD measures for all customers not covered by exemptions;
- must have systems to deal with identification issues in relation to those who cannot produce the standard evidence;
- must apply enhanced due diligence to take account of the greater potential for money laundering in higher risk cases, specifically when the customer is not physically present when being identified, and in respect of Politically Exposed Persons (PEPs) and correspondent banking (PEPs are individuals who hold, or have held, a senior political role and where there may be a greater risk of monies arising from corruption);
- some persons/entities must not be dealt with;
- must have specific policies in relation to the financially (and socially) excluded;
- if satisfactory evidence of identity is not obtained, the business relationship must not proceed further;
- must have some system for keeping customer information up-to-date.

2.2.5 Suspicious Activities and Reporting

The regulations require reports to be made of potential money laundering or terrorist financing activities.

Staff working in the financial sector are required to make reports:

- where they know; or
- where they suspect; or
- where they have reasonable grounds for knowing or suspecting, that a person is engaged in money laundering or terrorist financing.

Each firm is expected to provide a framework within which such suspicion reports may be raised and considered by a nominated officer, who may also be the MLRO. The nominated officer must consider each report and determine whether there are grounds for knowledge or suspicion for a report to be made to the Serious Organised Crime Agency (SOCA).

2.2.6   Staff Awareness and Training

The best designed control systems cannot operate effectively without staff who are alert to the risk of money laundering and who are trained in the identification of unusual activities or transactions which may prove to be suspicious.

Firms are therefore required to:

*   provide appropriate training to make staff aware of money laundering and terrorist financing issues and how these crimes might take place through the firm;
*   ensure staff are aware of the law, regulations and relevant criminal offences;
*   consider providing case studies and examples related to the firm's business;
*   train employees in how to operate a risk-based approach.

2.2.7   Record Keeping

Record keeping is an essential component of the audit trail that the money laundering regulations and FSA rules require to assist in any financial investigations.

Firms are therefore required to maintain appropriate systems for maintaining records and making these available when required and, in particular, should retain:

*   copies of the evidence obtained of a customer's identity for five years after the end of the customer relationship;
*   details of customer transactions for five years from the date of the transaction or five years from when the relationship with the customer ended whichever is the later;
*   details of actions taken in respect of internal and external suspicion reports;
*   details of information considered by the nominated officer in respect of an internal report where no external report is made.

3.   INSIDER DEALING

LEARNING OBJECTIVES

8.3.1   Know the offences that constitute insider dealing and the instruments covered

When directors or employees of a listed company buy or sell shares in that company, there is a possibility that they are committing a criminal act – insider dealing. For example, a director may be buying shares in the knowledge that the company's last six months of trade was better than the market expected. The director has the benefit of this information because he is 'inside' the company. Under the Criminal Justice Act 1993 this would be a criminal offence, punishable by a fine and/or a jail term.

To be found guilty of insider dealing, the Criminal Justice Act 1993 defines who is deemed to be an insider, what is deemed to be inside information and the situations that give rise to the offence.

Inside information is information that relates to particular securities or a particular issuer of securities (and not to securities or securities issuers generally) and:

*   is specific or precise;
*   has not been made public; and
*   if it were made public, would be likely to have a significant effect on the price of the securities.

This is generally referred to as 'unpublished price-sensitive information' and the securities are referred to as 'price-affected securities'.

The information becomes public when it is published, for example, a UK-listed company publishing price-sensitive news through the London Stock Exchange's Regulatory News Service. Information can be treated as public even though it may be acquired only by persons exercising diligence or expertise (for example, by careful analysis of published accounts, or by scouring a library).

A person has this price-sensitive information as an insider if he knows that it is inside information from an inside source. The person may have:

1. gained the information through being a director, employee or shareholder of an issuer of securities;
2. gained access to the information by virtue of his employment, office or profession (for example, the auditors to the company);
3. sourced the information from (1) or (2), either directly or indirectly.

The offence of insider dealing is committed when an insider acquires or disposes of price-affected securities while in possession of unpublished price-sensitive information. It is also an offence to encourage another person to deal in price-affected securities, or to disclose the information to another person (other than in the proper performance of employment). The acquisition or disposal must occur on a regulated market or through a professional intermediary.

The instruments covered by the insider dealing legislation in the Criminal Justice Act are described as 'securities'. For the purposes of this piece of law, securities are:

*   shares;
*   bonds (includes government bonds and others issued by a company or a public sector body);
*   warrants;
*   depositary receipts;
*   options (to acquire or dispose of securities);
*   futures (to acquire or dispose of securities);
*   contracts for differences (based on securities, interest rates or share indices).

Note that the definition of 'securities' does not embrace commodities and derivatives on commodities (such as options and futures on agricultural products, metals or energy products), or units/shares in open-ended collective investment schemes (such as OEICs, unit trusts and SICAVs).

4. MARKET ABUSE

LEARNING OBJECTIVES

8.3.2   Know the offences that constitute market abuse and the instruments
         covered

Market abuse is an offence introduced by the Financial Services and Markets Act 2000 (subsequently amended in the Market Abuse Directive 2005). It relates to behaviour by a person or a group of people working together, which occurs in relation to qualifying investments on a prescribed market that satisfies one or more of the following three conditions:

* The behaviour is based on information that is not generally available to those using the market and, if it were available, it would have an impact on the price.
* The behaviour is likely to give a false or misleading impression of the supply, demand or value of the investments concerned.
* The behaviour is likely to distort the market in the investments.

In all three cases the behaviour is judged on the basis of what a regular user of the market would view as a failure to observe the standards of behaviour normally expected in the market.

The Treasury has determined the 'qualifying investments' and 'prescribed markets' – broadly, they are the investments traded on any of the UK's Recognised Investment Exchanges (RIEs) such as the London Stock Exchange main market, AIM and PLUS Markets.

5. DATA PROTECTION ACT 1998

LEARNING OBJECTIVES

8.4.1   Understand the impact of the Data Protection Act 1998 on firms'
         activities

The Data Protection Act 1998 details how personal data should be dealt with to protect its integrity and to protect the rights of the persons concerned.

In order to comply with the Act, firms have a number of legal responsibilities, including:

* Notifying the Information Commissioner that it is processing information.
* To process personal information in accordance with the eight principles of the Data Protection Act.
* Answering subject access requests received from individuals.

Any firm that is holding and processing personal data is described as a Data Controller, and is required to comply with the Data Protection Act. The firm must be registered with the Information Commissioner.

The Data Protection Act lays down eight Data Protection Principles:

- Personal data shall be processed fairly and lawfully.
- Personal data shall be obtained for one or more specified and lawful purposes, and shall not be further processed in any manner that is incompatible with those purposes.
- Personal data shall be adequate, relevant and not excessive in relation to the purpose or purposes for which it is processed.
- Personal data shall be accurate and, where necessary, kept up-to-date.
- Personal data shall not be kept for longer than is necessary for its purpose or purposes.
- Personal data shall be processed in accordance with the rights of the subject under the Act.
- Appropriate technical and organisational measures shall be taken against unauthorised or unlawful processing of personal data, and against accidental loss or destruction of, or damage to the personal data.
- Personal data shall not be transferred to a country or territory outside the European Economic Area unless that country or territory ensures an adequate level of protection in relation to the processing of personal data.

Under these principles, firms are therefore required to take particular care if financial or medical information is held on a laptop or other portable device. Data should be encrypted and organisations must have policies on the appropriate use and security of portable devices and ensuring their staff are properly trained in these.

Other steps that can be taken to keep data safe include the following FSA recommendations:

- Employees should not have access to data beyond that necessary for them to perform their job. Where possible, data should be segregated and information, such as passport numbers, bank details and social security numbers, should be blanked out.
- You should look to monitor and control all flows of information in and out of the company.
- All forms of removable media should be disabled, except where there is a genuine business need. There should be no physical means available for unauthorised staff to remove information undetected.
- Where laptops or other portable devices are in use, these should be encrypted and wiped afterwards. Usage of such devices should be logged and monitored under the authority of an appropriate individual. Watertight policies using such devices should be in place.
- Software that tracks all activities, as well as web surfing and email traffic, should be installed on every single terminal on your network, and staff should be aware of this.
- Completely block access to all internet content that allows web-based communication. This includes all web-based email, messaging facilities on social networking sites, external instant messaging and 'peer-to-peer' file sharing software.
- Conduct due diligence of data security standards of your third party suppliers before contracts are agreed. Review this periodically. If you choose to outsource your IT, conduct checks on their staff also. After all, they have access to absolutely everything on your network.
- All visitors to your premises should be logged in and out, and be supervised while on site. Keep logs for a minimum of 12 months.

If a firm outsources, there are data protection implications. Firms must assess that the organisation can carry out the work in a secure way, check that they are doing so and take proper security measures. The firm must also have a written contract with the organisation that lays down how it can use and disclose the information entrusted to it.

6.   BREACHES, COMPLAINTS AND COMPENSATION

LEARNING OBJECTIVES

8.5.2   Know the responsibilities of the industry for handling customer complaints and dealing with breaches

6.1   Complaints

It is almost inevitable that customers will raise complaints against a firm providing financial services. Sometimes these complaints will be valid and sometimes not. The FSA requires authorised firms to deal with complaints from eligible complainants promptly and fairly. Eligible complainants are, broadly, individuals and small businesses.

The FSA requires firms to have appropriate written procedures for handling expressions of dissatisfaction from eligible complainants. However, the firm is able to apply these procedures to other complainants as well, if it so chooses. These procedures should be utilised regardless of whether the complaint is oral or written and whether the complaint is justified or not as long as it relates to the firm's provision or failure to provide a financial service.

These internal complaints handling procedures should provide for the receiving of complaints, acknowledgement of complaints in a timely manner, responding to those complaints, appropriately investigating the complaints and notifying the complainants of their right to go to the Financial Ombudsman Service (FOS) where relevant. Among other requirements, the complaints handling procedures must require the firm to issue its final response to the complainant. The final response must then follow within eight weeks of the date of the original complaint and the complainant must be notified of his/her right to refer their complaint to the FOS if he is dissatisfied with the firm's response.

The internal complaints handling procedures must make provision for the complaints to be investigated by an employee of sufficient competence who was not directly involved in the matter that is the subject of the complaint. The person charged with responding to the complaints must have the authority to settle the complaint, including offering redress where appropriate, or have access to someone with the necessary authority. The responses should adequately address the subject matter of the complaint and, where a complaint is upheld, to offer appropriate redress. Where the firm decides that redress is appropriate, the firm must provide the complainant with fair compensation for any acts or omissions for which it was responsible and comply with any offer of redress the complainant accepts. Any redress for financial loss should include consequential or prospective loss, in addition to actual loss.

The firm must take reasonable steps to ensure that all relevant employees (including any of the firm's appointed representatives) are aware of the firm's complaints handling procedures and endeavour to act in accordance with these.

6.2   Breaches and Complaints

LEARNING OBJECTIVES

8.5.1   Know the difference between a breach and a complaint

A 'breach' is any action (or inaction) which conflicts with regulatory requirements.

The term is most commonly used in relation to a breach of compliance rules, but the term is equally valid for all other regulations, such as a breach of HM Revenue & Customs rules relating to Individual Savings Accounts. Indeed, many firms will regard a failure to follow internal rules as a breach.

A breach is therefore a failure to follow rules and regulations, while a complaint is an expression of dissatisfaction by a customer. Needless to say, an investigation into a customer complaint may well reveal a breach of regulations or the firm's internal rules.

The purpose of recording breaches is both to ensure that corrective and preventative action can be taken and to determine whether the mistake needs to be reported to the FSA or another regulatory body. Recording can also be used to identify trends so that further corrective and preventative action can be considered and implemented. Breaches may be identified either through internal checks or through a customer complaint.

6.3   Financial Ombudsman Service (FOS)

LEARNING OBJECTIVES

8.5.3   Know the role of the Financial Ombudsman Service

Under the provisions of the Financial Services and Markets Act 2000, the FSA was given the power to make rules relating to the handling of complaints (in the previous section), and an independent body was established to administer and operate a dispute resolution scheme. It is funded by compulsory industry contributions.

The dispute resolution scheme is known as the Financial Ombudsman Service (FOS), designed to resolve complaints about financial services firms quickly and with minimum formality. Eligible complainants are able to refer complaints to the FOS where they are not satisfied with the response of the financial services firm. The decision of FOS is binding on firms, although not binding on the person making the complaint.

The Financial Ombudsman can require the firm to pay over money as a result of a complaint. This money award against the firm will be of such amount that the Ombudsman considers to be fair compensation; however, the sum cannot exceed £100,000. Where the decision is made to make a money award, the Ombudsman can award compensation for financial loss, pain and suffering, damage to reputation and distress or inconvenience.

6.4   Financial Services Compensation Scheme (FSCS)

LEARNING OBJECTIVES

8.5.4   Know the circumstances under which the financial services compensation scheme pays compensation and the compensation payable for investment claims

The Financial Services Compensation Scheme (FSCS) has been established to pay compensation or arrange continuing cover to eligible claimants in the event of a default by an authorised person. Default is, typically, the firm suffering insolvency. Eligible claimants are, broadly speaking, the less knowledgeable clients of the firm such as individuals and small organisations. These less knowledgeable clients are generally the firm's 'private customers' and exclude the more knowledgeable 'professional customers'. It is similar to an insurance policy that is paid for by all authorised firms and provides protection to some clients in the event of a firm collapsing. The claims could come from money on deposit with a bank, or claims in connection with investment business, such as the collapse of a fund manager or stockbroker.

The maximum level of compensation for claims against firms declared in default on or after 1 January 2010 is 100% of the first £50,000 per person per firm. Prior to that date, the maximum level of compensation for claims was 100% of the first £30,000 and 90% of the next £20,000 up to £48,000 per person per firm.

END OF CHAPTER QUESTIONS

Think of an answer for each question and refer to the appropriate section for confirmation.

Question	Answer Reference
1. What is the rationale behind the checks that the FSA undertakes to make sure that a firm is 'fit and proper' prior to authorisation?	Section 1.4
2. What are the five groups of controlled functions that require approved person status?	Section 1.5
3. If a firm disagrees with a decision of the FSA who can it appeal to?	Section 1.7
4. In what circumstances might simplified due diligence be appropriate?	Section 2.2.4
5. What is EDD and when might it be needed?	Section 2.2.4
6. What information should be kept in order to be compliant with the JMLSG guidance?	Section 2.2.7
7. What types of securities do the insider dealing rules apply to?	Section 3
8. What types of behaviour might lead to a charge of market abuse?	Section 4
9. What action should a firm take before it allows another firm to process customer data for it?	Section 5
10. If an authorised firm went bust, who could an investor seek compensation from?	Section 6.4

INVESTMENT WRAPPERS, TAX & TRUSTS

This syllabus area will provide approximately 8 of the 50 examination questions

In this chapter, we look at the main taxes that apply to individuals and then at the range of investment wrappers that are available and their tax attractiveness to investors.

We conclude with an overview of trusts and their uses.

1. TAXATION

LEARNING OBJECTIVES

9.1.1   Know the direct and indirect taxes as they apply to individuals: income tax; capital gains tax; inheritance tax; stamp duty and stamp duty reserve tax; VAT

9.1.2   Know the main exemptions in respect of the main personal taxes

In this section, we will review the main taxes that affect private individuals, with a focus on the impact of tax on investment income.

The main taxes that affect private investors are income tax, capital gains tax, stamp duty and inheritance tax.

1.1   Income Tax

Private investors are liable to pay tax on the income generated from their savings and investments. In this context, taxable income includes interest on bank deposits, the dividends payable on shares, income distributions paid by unit trusts and the interest on government stocks and corporate bonds.

Income from savings and investments is added to the investor's other income, such as salary or pension and income tax is charged on the total amount. Individuals have an annual personal allowance on which no tax is due and the rest is grouped into bands and taxed at different rates.

Tax is often deducted from interest and dividends before it is paid. How it is treated depends upon whether it is interest or dividends. In this context, dividends includes dividend payments from unit trusts and OEICs as well as from companies. Interest payments encompass bond interest payments and interest on cash deposits.

Interest income can be paid either gross or net, that is, either with tax deducted or without. For example, interest on bank deposits or other savings accounts is usually paid net of tax and will have 20% tax deducted. Interest on gilts can be paid either gross or net; if it is paid net, then it too will have tax at 20% deducted.

Dividends are paid net of tax. This includes dividends paid by companies and from investments in unit trusts and OEICs. You should note that unit trusts and OEICs that principally invest in bonds will pay an interest distribution and it is treated in the same way as other interest income.

How much tax is then due will depend upon what rate the investor pays tax at, as can be seen from the following table which shows the income tax rates and taxable bands for the 2009/10 tax years. These rates apply to income after the individual's personal allowance has been deducted.

	2009-10
Starting rate for savings: 10%	£0–£2,440
Basic rate: 20%	£0–£37,400
Higher rate: 40%	Over £37,400

As you can see from this, there is a 10% starting rate of tax which is for savings income only – savings income is the term used for interest. If non-savings income is above this limit then the 10% starting rate for savings will not apply. So, for example, if an individual has only savings income of say, £10,000 then the first £2,440 will be taxed at 10% and the balance at the basic rate. If the same person had non-savings income (say, a pension) of £5,000 then the band would not apply and the whole amount would be taxable at the basic rate.

In most cases, an individual will receive interest payments form which tax at 20% has been deducted and this will satisfy any liability to basic rate tax. A higher rate taxpayer will, however, face a further tax liability depending upon the rate of tax the pay. So, for example, an individual is a higher rate taxpayer and pays tax at 40%. He receives gross interest of £10,000 and tax will have been deducted at 20% so that the net payment to him is £8,000. He will be liable to pay tax at 40% on the gross amount amounting to £4,000 and can set off the tax already paid of £2,000 leaving him with a further liability of £2,000 to pay.

From 6 April 2010, a new higher band of tax becomes effective. Where an individual's income exceeds £150,000, the excess will be chargeable to income tax at 50%.

(Please note that details of the tax rates and bands have been included to explain how savings income is treated and you are not required to know these for the exam.)

With dividends the position is different.

When a company pays a dividend, it will do so from its net profits on which it will have paid corporation tax. Shareholders are the owners of the company and, recognising this, a credit for some of the tax already paid is given. This takes the form of a tax credit of 10% being applied to all dividends which can be used to offset any further liability to income tax that the shareholder may have.

So, for example, if an individual holds 1000 shares in a company which announces a dividend of 15p per share, when the dividend is paid the shareholder will receive a cheque for a net dividend of £150. Accompanying the dividend cheque will be a tax voucher which will show a tax credit of £16.66, that is £150 grossed up and then taxed at 10%. This tax credit can then be used to meet the income tax that is due.

The amount of income tax that will be due will depend on the rate of tax that the shareholder is liable to pay; this is where it differs significantly from how interest is taxed.

The rate of tax on dividends is 10% for income up to the basic rate limit. So, for an individual, other than a higher rate taxpayer, no further tax is due as the tax credit fully meets the tax liability that they are due to pay.

The position is completely different for higher rate taxpayers who will pay tax at either 32.5% or 42.5% depending upon whether their overall income exceeds £150,000 or not and so potentially some will be taxable at 32.5% and any balance over £150,000 at the new 42.5% rate. They can, however, set off the 10% tax credit against their liability which means there is either a further 22.5% tax or 32.5% tax due. Note that the additional amount of tax due is on the gross amount of the dividend.

1.2 Capital Gains Tax (CGT)

Capital Gains Tax (CGT) is a tax levied on an increase in the capital value of an asset; you normally only pay CGT when the asset is disposed of. For example, if an individual bought shares for £2,000 and later sold them for £17,000, then that individual has made a capital gain of £15,000.

CGT may be payable when an asset is sold or disposed of which includes when you:

- sell, give away, exchange, or transfer – 'dispose of' – all or part of an asset;
- receive a capital sum, such as an insurance payout for a damaged asset.

Most types of assets are liable to CGT and include items such as:

- shares;
- unit trusts;
- certain bonds;
- property (except your main home, or principal private residence).

As you can see from the list above, nearly all types of assets are caught by capital gains tax.

There are, however, a number of notable exemptions:

- Although property is chargeable to CGT, any gain on the sale of your main home is exempt. For CGT purposes, your main home is referred to as your 'principal private residence'.
- Gains on gilts and certain other sterling bonds, called 'qualifying corporate bonds', are exempt.
- Gains on assets held in accounts that benefit from tax exemptions, such as an ISA, Child Trust Fund or approved pension.
- Transfers between spouses.

In addition, individuals have an annual tax free allowance which is known as the annual exempt amount and which allows them to make a certain amount of gains tax-free each year.

For the tax year 2009/10, there is an annual tax free allowance of £10,100 and any net gains in excess are chargeable at a rate of 18%.

1.3   Inheritance Tax (IHT)

Inheritance Tax (IHT) is usually paid on the estate that someone leaves when they die. It is also sometimes payable on trusts or gifts made during someone's lifetime.

IHT is based on the value of assets that are transferred during the individual's lifetime or that are remaining at death, known as the estate of the deceased. Each individual has a nil rate band which is currently at £325,000 and any transfers in excess of the nil-rate band are then charged at 40%.

Inheritance tax is a complex area but some of the major exemptions are:

- assets left to the deceased person's spouse are exempt;
- assets left to registered charities are exempt;
- gifts made more than seven years before death can be exempt if certain conditions are met.

Since October 2007, it has also been possible to transfer any unused nil-rate band from a late spouse or civil partner to the second spouse or civil partner when they die. The percentage that is unused on the first death can then be used to reduce the IHT liability on the second death and can increase the inheritance tax threshold of the second partner from £325,000 to as much as £650,000 in 2009/10, depending on the circumstances.

1.4   Stamp Duty and Stamp Duty Reserve Tax (SDRT)

Stamp duty is a tax paid on share trades where a stock transfer form is used. SDRT is payable when an individual buys shares electronically and no stock transfer form is used. The rate is 0.5% of the purchase price and is paid only by the purchaser.

There is no stamp duty payable on the purchase of foreign shares, bonds, OEICs or unit trusts or on ETFs. However, for OEICs and unit trusts the fund will pay duty when it buys shares and the cost may be passed on to the investor in the difference between the buying and selling price.

1.5   Value Added Tax (VAT)

VAT is chargeable by firms and individuals whose turnover exceeds a certain amount, when they supply what are known as taxable goods or services. Although this affects all firms except those below the VAT threshold, they are allowed to deduct tax they have paid on purchases, so reducing their liability.

VAT is payable normally at 17.5%. It is relevant to a number of investment services. For example, fees charged for providing an investment management service to an Authorised Unit Trust (AUT) would be VAT-exempt, while those charged to clients (eg, private individuals) would be VATable. There are also exceptions where no VAT is payable, such as with brokers commission for the execution of a stock market trade.

2. INVESTMENT WRAPPERS

As part of their economic policies, many governments wish to encourage both savings and share ownership.

One of the ways this is achieved in the UK is by giving tax advantages to make certain savings and investment products attractive to savers and investors alike.

Some of the principal schemes available are known as investment 'wrappers': the term includes products such as ISAs, Child Trust Funds (CTFs), pensions and investment bonds.

As a result of their attractiveness, they are subject to a range of rules prescribing areas such as, who can invest, the amount of annual contributions that can be made and what are permissible investments. These rules are made by HM Revenue & Customs (HMRC).

3. INDIVIDUAL SAVINGS ACCOUNTS (ISAs)

LEARNING OBJECTIVES

9.2.1   Know the definition of and aim of ISAs

9.2.2   Know the tax incentives provided by ISAs

9.2.3   Know the types of ISA available

9.2.4   Know the eligibility conditions for investors

9.2.5   Know the following aspects of investing in ISAs: subscriptions, transfers, withdrawals, number of managers, number of accounts.

3.1 What is an ISA?

An ISA is an acronym for 'Individual Savings Account'. The ISA itself is often referred to as an investment wrapper because it is essentially an account that holds other investments, such as deposits, shares, OEICs and unit trusts and allows them to be invested in a tax-efficient manner.

Their tax advantages have made them very popular and, as at 5 April 2008, £142 billion was held in cash ISAs and £78 billion in stocks & shares ISAs.

Firms offering investments in ISAs, such as banks, building societies and fund management companies, must be approved by HMRC. The approved entity is known as the 'ISA manager'.

HMRC is also responsible for setting the detailed rules applicable to ISAs.

3.2   Eligibility

Stocks and shares ISAs are available only to residents of the UK over the age of 18. Cash ISAs are available to those aged 16 or over.

3.3   Tax Position

ISAs were set up by the government to encourage individual investment. The particular incentive for investment was that the investments held within an ISA were free of:

- income tax; and
- Capital Gains Tax (CGT).

This changed from 6 April 2005, when the government withdrew part of the tax advantage; it is now no longer possible to reclaim the tax credit on dividends paid on shares held within an ISA. However, the tax advantage remains for investments earning interest, such as cash deposits and government and corporate bonds. They are also still attractive for higher rate taxpayers who are not liable to any additional income tax on interest or dividends.

3.4   Types of ISA

Over the years, the rules surrounding the types of ISA had become complex and this made them less than straightforward for investors to understand and have caused firms difficulties in administering them.

As a result, the government has simplified the rules and there is now simply an ISA and savers are able to contribute to two components:

- cash;
- stocks and shares.

Under these new rules, savers are able to hold one of each component per year, with either the same or different providers. In the year when a subscription is made, therefore, an investor can open an ISA to hold the cash component with one manager and a separate one to hold the stocks and shares component with another. So, for example, an investor cannot open an ISA to hold part of the cash component and then later in the year open one with another manager to hold the balance; it must all be with one manager. The same is the case for the stocks and shares component.

3.5   Subscription Limits

Every eligible investor has an annual ISA investment allowance known as a subscription limit.

Changes to the subscription limits to ISAs were announced as part of the 2009 budget which will see increases in the amounts that can be subscribed but which are phased over two tax years.

The existing ISA regulations stipulate that the overall annual subscription limit for an ISA is £7,200 of which up to £3,600 can be saved in a Cash ISA with one provider. The remainder can be invested in stocks and shares with either the same or another provider.

Individuals who are aged 50 and over in 2009/10 will have an increased allowance with effect from 6 October 2009. From that date the ISA limit will be raised to £10,200 of which £5,100 can be held in cash.

All ISA investors will be able to take advantage of the new limits from 6 April 2010.

3.6   Transfers

Investors are able to transfer an existing ISA from one manager to another manager provided that the receiving manager is prepared to accept it. Transfers can be whole or just part. Transfers of the same year's subscriptions, however, must be for the full amount.

Since April 2008, savers are able to transfer some or all of the money saved in previous years from cash ISAs to stocks and shares ISAs without affecting their annual ISA investment allowance.

It will also be possible to transfer money saved in the current tax year in cash ISAs to stocks and shares ISAs. Such transfers must be the whole amount saved in that tax year in that cash ISA up to the day of the transfer. The individual is then able to save up to the full remaining balance of their annual ISA investment allowance in ISAs in that tax year.

For example, if an individual has invested £2,000 into a cash ISA at the beginning of the tax year, he/she can transfer that amount to a stocks and shares ISA before the end of the tax year. The cash ISA is then treated as if it had never existed. The individual could then make further investments into the stocks and shares ISA of £5,200 which along with his/her initial investment would fully use up his/her annual allowance.

It should be noted that whilst a transfer from a cash ISA to a stocks and shares ISA can be made, a transfer the opposite way round cannot be made.

3.7   Withdrawals

Withdrawals of any cash or investments from an ISA are permanent. Once withdrawn they cannot be re-deposited. The only way in which funds can be added to an ISA is by using the current year's subscription. For example, if an investor withdraws funds from their cash ISA they cannot change their mind later and redeposit all or part of the amount if they have already used their current year's subscription.

4.   CHILD TRUST FUNDS (CTFs)

LEARNING OBJECTIVES

9.3.1   Know the tax benefits to a child on the maturity of a child trust fund

9.3.2   Know the main characteristics of child trust funds

The Child Trust Fund (CTF) has been introduced by the government to help and encourage parents to save for their child's future.

The government's intention is that when the child reaches 18, they will have some money to give them a start to life as an adult. At 18, they can carry on saving or use the money for other things – like driving lessons or training courses.

The main characteristics of the CTF are as follows:

- It is a long-term savings and investment account that is available to children born on or after 1 September 2002.
- Money invested in a CTF belongs to the child and cannot be withdrawn until the child turns 18.
- The government gives a £250 voucher to each eligible child to start the CTF. As with ISAs, the tax credit on dividends cannot, however, be reclaimed.
- Children from lower income families will receive an extra £250.
- Parents, relatives and friends can, between them, add up to a further £1,200 a year to the CTF.
- At age seven, the government makes a further payment of £250, with children from lower income families receiving £500.
- There will be no tax on any interest or gains made on the money in the CTF.
- At 16, the child will be able to manage his CTF account, for example by deciding to change provider or type of account.
- At 18, young people with CTF accounts will be able to decide for themselves how best to use the money.
- CTFs are treated in the same way as ISAs in respect of tax benefits.

Providers offer up to three forms of CTF account: a savings account, an account that invests in shares or a stakeholder account. The savings account is a deposit account and offers a secure type of investment but one whose value will be affected by inflation. The accounts that invest in shares offer the potential for growth, but the risk of falling in value. The stakeholder accounts invest in shares but the government has set certain rules to reduce risk – in particular, when the child reaches the age of 13, the money starts to be moved from shares into safer investments.

Other types of account are also available, such as Sharia'a accounts and ethical accounts.

The first CTF accounts will mature in 2020 and if the child does not take the money out it will automatically rollover into an ISA on maturity. The aim is to encourage young people to maintain a saving habit into adulthood.

5. PENSIONS

LEARNING OBJECTIVES

9.4.1   Know the tax incentives provided by pensions

5.1   Retirement Planning

For many people their pension and their house are their main assets.

A pension is an investment fund where contributions are made, usually during the individual's working life, to provide a lump sum on retirement plus an annual pension payable thereafter. Pension contributions are tax-effective, as tax relief is given on contributions.

Some of the main tax incentives of pensions include:

- Tax relief on contributions made by individuals and employers.
- Pension funds are not subject to income tax and CGT and so the pension fund can grow tax-free.
- The ability to take a pension from age 55.
- An option to take a tax free lump sum of at retirement.
- The option to include death benefits as part of the scheme.

These tax advantages were put in place by the government to encourage people to provide for their old age. Pensions are subject to income tax when they are received.

One of the earliest kinds of scheme supplementing state-funding was the occupational pension scheme. In an occupational pension scheme, the employer makes pension contributions on behalf of its workers. For example, an occupational pension scheme might provide an employee with 1/40th of his/her final salary for every year of service, the employee could then retire with an annual pension the size of which was related to the number of years' service. This type of occupational pension scheme is known as a final salary scheme or defined benefit scheme. Employers have generally stopped providing such occupational schemes to new employees because of rising life expectancies and volatile investment returns, and the implications these factors have on the funding requirement for defined benefit schemes.

Instead, occupational pension schemes are now typically provided to new employees on a defined contribution basis – where the size of the pension is driven by the contributions paid and the investment performance of the fund. Under this type of scheme, an investment fund is built up and the amount of pension that will be received at retirement will be determined by the value of the fund and the amount of pension it can generate.

In the 1980s the government began to encourage people to make individual provision for their retirement, potentially by setting up their own personal pension.

Yet further changes were made in 2006 with a major overhaul of pension rules and associated taxation. 'A' day, as it was known, brought about much more flexibility in contributions which attract tax relief for members. Tax rules have also been harmonised between the different types of registered (ie, approved) schemes.

Pensions are becoming increasingly important as people live longer and commentators speak of a 'pensions time bomb', where the pension provided by the state, the individuals and their employers will be inadequate to meet the needs in retirement. As an example, it is predicted that by 2040 over 50% of the people in the UK will be over 65. When the state pension was introduced in the UK, the initial need was funding for the rare event of people living beyond the age of 65. Today this is very common.

As a result, the government is implementing wide-ranging reforms based legally on recommendations by Lord Turner's pension commission. Key changes already agreed include:

*   The state pension age for women will gradually increase for those born on or after 6 April 1950 but before 6 April 1955, so that it will eventually be the same as that of a man born on the same date, in other words at age 65.
*   Men and women born on or after 6 April 1955 but before 6 April 1959 have a State Pension age of 65.
*   The age of eligibility for the state pensions to rise to:
    *   66 for both men and women over a two-year period from 2024;
    *   67 over two years from 2034; and
    *   68 in two years from 2044.
*   Rises in the state pension and the 'guarantee' element of pensions credit to be linked to rises in average earnings at some point after 2012.
*   From 2010, the National Insurance contributions needed to get a full basic state pension will be cut to 30 years for men born after 5 April 1945 and women born after 5 April 1950.

Legislation presented to parliament in December 2007 proposes that from 2012, workers not in a company scheme will be automatically enrolled into either an existing good scheme or into a new national pension savings scheme (Personal Accounts). The worker will contribute 4%, the employer 3% and the government, through tax relief, will result in 1%. Personal Accounts will also be open to others, such as the self-employed. The date for its introduction has since slipped and it will now be introduced on a phased basis from 2014.

5.2 Types of Pension Schemes

9.4.2   Know the basic characteristics of the following: state pension scheme; occupational pension schemes; personal pensions including self invested personal pensions (SIPPs)/small self-administered schemes (SSAS); stakeholder pensions

5.2.1 State Pension Scheme

The state pension comes in two parts:

*   Basic State Pension;
*   Additional State Pension or State Second Pension.

State pensions are provided out of current National Insurance contributions, with no investment for future needs. This is a problem as dependency ratios (the proportion of working people to retired people) are forecast to fall from 4:1 in 2002 to 3:1 by 2030 and 2.5:1 by 2050. This means that by 2050 either each worker will have to support almost twice as many retired people, or the support per head will need to fall substantially, or some combination of these changes.

Currently, the State Pension is payable from age 65 for men and 60 for women. The pension age for women is being gradually increased so that the pension age for both men and women will be 65 from 6 April 2020, when everyone will draw their pensions at the same age.

The Basic State Pension is paid at a flat rate to people who have made National Insurance contributions during their working life. Even if people have had long periods of unemployment or invalidity, which might mean that they are not entitled to a full pension, there is provision for the amount of Basic State Pension to which an individual may be entitled to be topped up through a system known as the Pension Credit Guarantee. The Pensions Credit Guarantee is a means tested benefit that is also available to those in receipt of a full basic state pension.

The Additional State Pension or State Second Pension – also known as 'S2P' – was previously known as the State Earnings Related Pensions (SERPS) until 2002. SERPS was earnings related – the higher the earnings, the bigger the pension. It was reformed in 2002 to become the State Second Pension to provide a more generous additional state pension for those on low to moderate income levels and certain carers and disabled individuals and is earnings related.

Workers can 'contract out' of the State Second Pension scheme and put more into their occupational pension scheme, personal pension scheme or stakeholder scheme (see below). Workers who 'contract out' by joining their employer's contracted-out occupational pension scheme pay reduced National Insurance contributions that should enable them to pay more into their pension scheme.

5.2.2   Occupational Pension Schemes

Occupational pension schemes are run by companies for their employees. The advantages of these schemes are:

- Employers must contribute to the fund (some pension schemes do not involve any contributions from the employee – these are called non-contributory schemes).
- Running costs are often lower than for personal schemes and the costs are often met by the employer.
- The employer must ensure the fund is well run and for defined benefit schemes must make up any shortfall in funding.

The occupational pension scheme could take the form of a defined benefit scheme, also known as a 'final salary scheme', where the pension received is related to the number of years of service and the individual's final salary.

Alternatively, it could take the form of a defined contribution scheme, where the pension provided is related to the contributions made and investment performance achieved.

The higher cost of providing a defined benefit scheme is part of the reason why many companies have closed their defined benefit schemes to new joiners and make only defined contribution schemes available to staff. Over half of the defined benefit schemes have closed to new joiners since 2001 as the stock market decline has caused companies problems with the under funding of their schemes. A key advantage of defined contribution schemes for employers over defined benefit schemes is that poor performance is not the employer's problem; it is the employee who will end up with a smaller pension.

Occupational pension schemes are structured as trusts, with the investment portfolio managed by professional asset managers. The asset managers are appointed by, and report to, the trustees of the scheme. The trustees will typically include representatives from the company (eg, company directors) as well as employee representatives.

5.3   Private Pensions or Personal Pensions

Private pensions or personal pensions are individual pension plans. They are defined contribution schemes that might be used by employees of companies which do not run their own scheme or where employees opt out of the company scheme or in addition to an existing pension scheme and by the self-employed. Many employers actually organise personal pension schemes for their employees, by arranging the administration of these schemes with an insurance company or an asset management firm. Such employers may also contribute to the personal pension schemes of their employees.

Employees and the self-employed who wish to provide for their pension and do not have access to occupational schemes or employer arranged personal pensions, have to organise their own personal pension schemes. These will often be arranged through an insurance company or an asset manager, where the individual can choose from the variety of investment funds offered.

Individuals also have the facility to run a Self-Invested Personal Pension (SIPP), commonly administered by a stockbroker or IFA on their behalf. In a SIPP, it is the individual who decides which investments are included in the scheme, subject to HMRC guidelines.

Smaller companies can also make independent pension arrangements by setting up a Small Self Administered Scheme (SSAS). Under these schemes, the directors keep full control of the scheme and decide, within limits, the size and timing of contributions and, as their own trustees, they keep full control of the investments. They are required to have a pensioner trustee who is independent of the company and who is responsible for ensuring that investments are made in accordance with HMRC regulations. The powers open to the trustees mean that the pension fund's fortunes may be tightly bound to those of the company. For this reason they are usually suitable only for the directors and their family.

The schemes are approved by HMRC which means that they are tax-exempt. The contributions are tax-deductible and there is no tax either on investment income or capital gains. Although there is no further tax due, the tax credit on any dividends received cannot be reclaimed.

In a private scheme the key responsibility that lies with the individual is that the individual chooses the investment fund in a scheme administered by an insurance company or asset manager, or the actual investments in a SIPP. It is then up to the individual to monitor the performance of his investments and assess whether it will be sufficient for his retirement needs.

5.4   Stakeholder Pensions

A stakeholder pension is simply a type of personal pension that incurs low charges. It is available from a range of financial services companies, such as banks, insurance companies and building societies.

Stakeholder pensions must satisfy a number of minimum government standards to ensure that they offer value for money and flexibility, including:

- **Low charges** – for people who joined a stakeholder pension scheme on or after 6 April 2005, the cap is an annual management charge of 1.5% for the first ten years, which will reduce to 1%, from ten years onwards if these members remain in the scheme.
- **Low and flexible contributions** – the minimum contribution cannot be greater than £20, and there cannot be a requirement for regular monthly contribution.
- **Transferability** – there must be no charges for transfer to another scheme.
- **Default option** – pension funds can allocate funds between different kinds of investment. A stakeholder scheme must provide a default for those unwilling to choose their own allocation between, say, UK shares, overseas shares or bond funds.

HOTSPOT

9

Go online to your elearning product for further information on pensions.

If you haven't purchased your elearning product, you can order now by calling Client Services on +44(0)20 7645 0680.

6.   INVESTMENT BONDS

LEARNING OBJECTIVES

9.5.1   Know the tax incentives provided by investment bonds – onshore/ offshore

9.5.2   Know the main characteristics of investment bonds

An investment bond is a single premium life assurance policy that is taken out for the purposes of investment. It is a common form of investment in the UK as it has received favourable tax treatment from governments interested in promoting savings and investment. The potential favourable treatment has been made more complex with the reduction in the capital gains tax to 18% in 2008, when comparing investment bonds with other types of investments, such as OEICs or unit trusts. A case-by-case analysis will now be required, taking into account the investors' risk appetite, cash flow needs and the investor's marginal income tax rates at the time of the investment. In the right circumstances, however, investment bonds can still receive favourable tax treatment.

They are issued by insurance companies and may be linked to one or more of the insurance company's unit linked investment funds.

They are structured in various ways in order to provide either capital growth or a regular income to investors. There is a wide range of investment bonds available including:

- with-profit investment bonds;
- distribution bonds;
- guaranteed equity bonds;
- unit-linked bonds.

Within these bonds, the investor will have a choice of investment fund with differing levels of risk, geographic coverage and investment style.

They will usually have a choice of two basic charging structures: an initial charge structure and an establishment charge structure. An initial charge involves all of the costs being taken up front, while the other spreads the costs, usually over the first five years. There may also be exit charges for early encashment.

Investment bonds can be a very useful tool for tax planning purposes.

Up to 5% of the original investment can be taken from an investment bond each year for 20 years without incurring an immediate tax liability. Also, if the 5% is not taken at the beginning of the investment bond's life, it can be rolled up on a cumulative basis and taken at a later stage, again without an immediate tax liability.

When investment bonds are encashed, the profits made are taxed as income rather than capital gains. As a result, basic rate tax-payers would not be liable to any tax on the proceeds of the bond, providing that the withdrawal does not push them into the higher rate tax band. Higher rate taxpayers are currently liable to tax at their higher rate less the basic rate (for example, a 40% taxpayer can deduct the basic rate of 20% to leave a further 20% liability) on policy gains.

The ability to defer any tax liability until encashment makes investment bonds particularly attractive to higher rate taxpayers who know that they will become basic rate taxpayers at some point in the future. This means that during the lifetime of the bond they can make withdrawals and defer the liability on any tax until the policy is encashed. If at the time of encashment the policyholders have become basic rate taxpayers, then there is a good chance that they will incur no tax liability.

Investment bonds are also issued by life assurance companies based in tax havens such as the Channel Islands. The structure of these bonds is similar to the ones available in the UK but their tax treatment differs. A notable difference is that income tax is charged at the full rates and so a basic rate taxpayer faces a 20% charge and a higher rate taxpayer will pay tax at a full 40 or 50%.

7.   TRUSTS

LEARNING OBJECTIVES

9.6.1   Know the features of the main trusts: discretionary; interest in possession; bare

9.6.2   Know the definition of the following terms: trustee; settlor; beneficiary

9.6.3   Know the main reasons for creating trusts

7.1   What is a Trust?

A trust is the legal means by which one person gives property to another person to look after on behalf of yet another individual or a set of individuals.

Starting with the individuals involved, the person who creates the trust is known as the 'settlor'. The person he gives the property to, to look after on behalf of others is called the 'trustee' and the individuals for whom it is intended are known as the 'beneficiaries'.

7.2   Uses of Trusts

Trusts are widely used in estate and tax planning for high net worth individuals and are encountered throughout retail investment firms from execution-only stockbrokers to private banks.

Some of their main uses include:

- To provide funds for a specific purpose, such as the maintenance of young children.
- To set aside funds for disabled or incapacitated children in order to protect and provide for their financial maintenance.

- To reduce future inheritance tax liabilities by transferring assets into a trust and so out of the settlor's ownership.
- To separate out rights to income and capital so that, for example, the spouse of a second marriage receives the income during his/her life and the capital passes on that person's death to the settlor's children.

Trusts are also the underlying structure for many major investment vehicles, such as pension funds, charities and unit trusts.

7.3   Types of Trusts

There are four main types of trust:

- **Bare or absolute trusts** – where a trustee holds assets for one or more persons absolutely.
- **Interest in possession trusts** – where a beneficiary has a right to the income of the trust during his/her life and the capital passes to others on their death.
- **Accumulation trusts** – where the trustees have discretion whether trust income can be accumulated or paid out but only for a certain period, after which a beneficiary will become entitled to either the income or capital at a certain date in the future.
- **Discretionary trusts** – where the trustees have discretion to whom the capital and income is paid, within certain criteria.

END OF CHAPTER QUESTIONS

Think of an answer for each question and refer to the appropriate section for confirmation.

Question		Answer Reference
1.	What additional rates of tax will be paid on a dividend by a higher rate taxpayer?	Section 1.1
2.	What assets are liable to CGT?	Section 1.2
3.	At what rate is CGT payable?	Section 1.2
4.	How does the eligibility for an ISA differ between a cash ISA and a stock and shares ISA?	Section 3.2
5.	What is the annual ISA allowance and how much of this can be invested in a cash ISA?	Section 3.4
6.	What happens to a CTF on maturity?	Section 4
7.	How much can be invested annually in a CTF?	Section 4
8.	What is the key difference between a defined benefit scheme and a defined contribution scheme?	Section 5.2.2
9.	How much can be withdrawn from an investment bond each year without triggering an income tax charge?	Section 6
10.	What is the type of trust where a trustee holds assets for another person absolutely?	Section 7.3

CHAPTER TEN

OTHER RETAIL FINANCIAL PRODUCTS

This syllabus area will provide approximately 3 of the 50 examination questions

In this final chapter, we look at other retail financial products, including loans, mortgages and life assurance.

1. LOANS

LEARNING OBJECTIVES

10.1.1   Know the differences between bank loans, overdrafts and credit card borrowing

10.1.4   Know the difference between secured and unsecured borrowing

1.1   Loans and Overdrafts

Individuals can borrow money from banks and building societies in three main ways:

- overdrafts;
- credit card borrowing;
- loans.

1.1.1   Overdrafts

When an individual draws out more money than he holds in his current account, he becomes overdrawn. His account is described as being in overdraft.

If the amount overdrawn is within a limit previously agreed with the bank, the overdraft is said to be authorised. If it has not been previously agreed, or exceeds the agreed limit, it is unauthorised.

Unauthorised overdrafts are very expensive, usually incurring both a high rate of interest on the borrowed money and a fee. The bank may refuse to honour cheques written on an unauthorised overdrawn account, commonly referred to as 'bouncing' cheques.

Authorised overdrafts agreed with the bank in advance are charged interest at a lower rate. Some banks allow small overdrafts without charging fees to avoid infuriating a customer who might be overdrawn by a relatively low amount.

Overdrafts are a convenient but expensive way of borrowing money and borrowers should try to restrict their use to temporary periods and avoid unauthorised overdrafts as far as possible.

1.1.2   Credit Cards

Customers in the UK are very attached to their 'flexible friends' – a typical pet name for credit cards from savings institutions like banks and building societies and other cards from retail stores known as store cards. In other countries, including much of Europe, the use is much less widespread.

A wide variety of retail goods such as food, electrical goods, petrol and cinema tickets can be paid for using a credit card. The retailer is paid by the credit card company for the goods sold, the credit card company charges the retailer a small fee, but this enables the store to sell goods to customers using their credit cards.

Customers are typically sent a monthly statement by the credit card company. Customers can then choose to pay all the money owed to the credit card company, or just a percentage of the total sum owed. Interest is charged on the balance owed by the customer.

Generally, the interest rate charged on credit cards is relatively high compared to other forms of borrowing, including overdrafts. However, if a credit card customer pays the full balance each month, he is borrowing interest-free. It is also common for credit card companies to offer 0% interest to new customers for balances transferred from other cards and for new purchases for a set period, often six months. These offers are often, however, only available if a fee is paid.

1.1.3 Loans

Loans can be subdivided into two groups:

* secured loans; and
* unsecured loans.

Unsecured loans are typically used to purchase consumer goods. Another example is a student loan to be repaid after university.

The lender will check the credit worthiness of the borrower – assessing whether he can afford to repay the loan and interest over the agreed term of, say, 48 months from his income given his existing outgoings.

The unsecured loan is not linked to the item that is purchased with the loan (in contrast to mortgages which are covered below), so if the borrower defaults it can be difficult for the lender to enforce repayment.

The usual mechanism for the unsecured lender to enforce repayment is to start legal proceedings to get the money back.

In contrast, if secured loans are not repaid the lender can repossess the specific property which was the security for the loan.

EXAMPLE:

Jenny borrows £500,000 to buy a house.

The loan is secured on the property. Jenny loses her job and is unable to continue to meet the repayments and interest.

Because the loan is secured, the lender is able to take the house to recoup the money. If the lender takes this route, the house will be sold and the lender will take the amount owed and give the rest, if any, to Jenny.

As seen in this example, it is common for loans made to buy property to be secured. Such loans are referred to as mortgages and the security provided to the lender means that the rate of interest is likely to be lower than on other forms of borrowing, like overdrafts and unsecured loans.

1.2   Interest Rates

LEARNING OBJECTIVES

10.1.2   Know the difference between the quoted interest rate on borrowing and the effective annual rate of borrowing

10.1.3   Be able to calculate the effective annual rate of borrowing, given the quoted interest rate and frequency of payment

The costs of borrowing vary depending on the form of borrowing, how long the money is required for, the security offered and the amount borrowed.

Mortgages, secured on a house, are much cheaper than credit cards and authorised overdrafts. Unauthorised overdrafts will incur high rates of interest plus charges.

Borrowers also have to grapple with the different rates quoted by lenders; loan companies traditionally quote flat rates that are lower than the true rate or effective annual rate.

EXAMPLE

The Moneybags Credit Card Company might quote its interest rate at 12% per annum, charged on a quarterly basis.

The effective annual rate can be determined by taking the quoted rate and dividing by four (to represent the quarterly charge). It is this rate that is applied to the amount borrowed on a quarterly basis. 12% divided by 4 = 3%.

Imagine an individual borrows £100 on his/her Moneybags credit card, assuming he makes no repayments for a year how much will be owed?

At the end of the first quarter £100 x 3% = £3 will be added to the balance outstanding, to make it £103.

At the end of the second quarter, interest will be due on both the original borrowing and the interest. In other words there will be interest charged on the first quarter's interest of £3, as well as the £100 original borrowing. £103 x 3% = £3.09 will be added to make the outstanding balance £106.09.

At the end of the third quarter interest will be charged at 3% on the amount outstanding (including the first and second quarters' interest). £106.09 x 3% = £3.18 will be added to make the outstanding balance £109.27.

At the end of the fourth quarter interest will be charged at 3% on the amount outstanding (including the first, second and third quarters' interest). £109.27 x 3% = £3.28 will be added to make the outstanding balance £112.55.

In total the interest incurred on the £100 was £12.55 over the year. This is an effective annual rate of 12.55/100 x 100 = 12.55%.

There is a shortcut method to arrive at the effective annual rate seen above. It is simply to take the quoted rate, divide by the appropriate frequency (four for quarterly, two for half-yearly, 12 for monthly) and express the result as a decimal – in other words 3% will be expressed as 0.03, 6% as 0.06 etc.

The decimal is then added to 1, and multiplied by itself by the appropriate frequency. The result minus 1, and multiplied by 100 is the effective annual rate.

From the above example:

- 12% divided by 4 = 3%, expressed as 0.03.
- 1 + 0.03 = 1.03.
- 1.03^4 = 1.03 x 1.03 x 1.03 x 1.03 = 1.1255.
- 1.1255 – 1 = 0.1255 x 100 = 12.55%.

To make comparisons easier, lenders must quote the true cost of borrowing, embracing the effective annual rate and including any fees that are required to be paid by the borrower. This is known as Annual Percentage Rate (APR). The additional fees that the lender adds to the cost of borrowing might be loan arrangement fees.

The formula above can also be applied to deposits to determine the effective rate of a deposit paying interest at regular intervals.

2.   PROPERTY AND MORTGAGES

LEARNING OBJECTIVES

10.2.1   Understand the characteristics of the mortgage market: interest rates

2.1   Characteristics of the Property Market and Mortgages

In the UK the proportion of families who own, or are buying, their home is higher than in many other countries in the European Union. As well as buying their own home, some have taken out second mortgages to buy holiday homes in areas like Cornwall, France and Spain, while others have taken out a 'buy-to-let' mortgage loan with a view to letting a property out to tenants.

Because of the past performance of property prices, property came to be seen as a reasonably safe investment. The recent crash in the property market has provided a salutary reminder that prices can go down as well as up.

The purchase of a property will typically be financed by a mortgage. A mortgage is simply a secured loan, with the security taking the form of a property.

A mortgage is typically provided to finance the purchase of that property and for most people their main form of borrowing is the mortgage on their house or flat. Mortgages tend to be taken out over a long term, with most mortgages running for 20 or 25 years.

Whether a mortgage is to buy a house or flat, or to 'buy-to-let', the factors considered by the lender are much the same. The mortgage lender, such as the building society or bank, will consider each application for a loan in terms of the credit risk – the risk of not being repaid the principal sum loaned and the interest due.

Applicants are assessed in terms of:

- Income and security of employment.
- Existing outgoings – utility bills, other household expenses, school fees etc.
- The size of the loan in relation to the value of the property being purchased.

A second mortgage is sometimes taken out on a single property. If the borrower defaults on his borrowings, the first mortgage ranks ahead of the second one in terms of being repaid out of the proceeds of the property sale.

There are four main methods by which the interest on a mortgage may be charged. These are:

- variable rate;
- fixed rate;
- capped rate; and
- tracker rate.

In a standard variable rate mortgage the borrower pays interest at a rate that varies with prevailing interest rates. The lender's standard variable rates will reflect increases or decreases in the rates set by the Bank of England. Once he has entered into a variable rate mortgage, the borrower will benefit from rates falling and remaining low, but will suffer the additional costs when rates increase.

In a fixed rate mortgage the borrower's interest rate is set for an initial period, usually the first three or five years. If interest rates rise the borrower is protected from the higher rates throughout this period, continuing to pay the lower, fixed rate of interest. However, if rates fall, and perhaps stay low, the fixed rate loan can only be cancelled if a redemption penalty is paid. The penalty is calculated to recoup the loss suffered by the lender as a result of the cancellation of the fixed rate loan. It is common for fixed rate borrowers to be required to remain with the lender and pay interest at the lender's standard variable rate for a couple of years after the fixed rate deal ends – commonly referred to as a 'lock in' period.

Capped mortgages protect borrowers from rates rising above a particular rate – the 'capped rate'. For example, a mortgage might be taken out at 6%, with the interest rate based on the lender's standard variable rate, but with a cap at 7%. If prevailing rates fall to 5% the borrower pays at that rate, but if rates rise to 8% the rate paid cannot rise above the cap, and is only 7%.

A tracker mortgage is one that is linked to another rate such as the Bank of England base rate. The tracker rate will be set at a percentage above the Bank of England base rate, say 1% above, and will then increase or decrease as base rate changes hence why it is called a tracker.

2.2   Types of Mortgage

LEARNING OBJECTIVES

10.2.2   Know the definition of and types of mortgage: repayment; interest only

2.2.1   Repayment Mortgages

The most straightforward form of mortgage is a repayment mortgage. This is simply a mortgage where the borrower will make monthly payments to the lender, with each monthly payment comprising both interest and capital.

EXAMPLE

Mr Mullergee borrows £100,000 from XYZ Bank to finance the purchase of a flat on a repayment basis over 25 years. Each month he is required to pay £600 to XYZ Bank.

In the above example, Mr Mullergee will pay in total £180,000 to XYZ Bank (£600 x 12 months x 25 years), a total of £80,000 interest over and above the capital borrowed of £100,000.

Each payment he makes will be partly allocated to interest and partly allocated to capital. In the early years the payments are predominantly interest. Towards the middle of the term the capital begins to reduce significantly and at the end of the mortgage term the payments are predominantly capital.

The key advantage of a repayment mortgage over other forms of mortgage is that, as long as the borrower meets the repayments each month, he is guaranteed to pay off the loan over the term of the mortgage.

The main risks attached to a repayment mortgage from the borrower's perspective are:

- The cost of servicing the loan could increase, where interest is charged at the lender's standard variable rate of interest. This rate of interest will increase if interest rates go up. Mortgage repayments can rise significantly at the end of a fixed rate deal when they revert to the standard variable rate.
- The borrower runs the risk of having the property repossessed if he fails to meet the repayments – remember the mortgage loan is secured on the underlying property. These risks also apply to other forms of mortgage.

2.2.2 Interest-Only Mortgages

As the name suggests, an interest-only mortgage requires the borrower to make interest payments to the lender throughout the period of the loan. At the same time the borrower generally puts money aside each month, into some form of investment.

The borrower's aim is for the investment to grow through regular contributions and investment returns (such as dividends, interest and capital growth) so that at the end of the mortgage the accumulated investment is sufficient to pay back the capital borrowed and perhaps offer some additional cash.

EXAMPLE

Ms Ward borrows £100,000 from XYZ Bank to finance the purchase of a flat on an interest-only basis over 25 years. Each month she is required to pay £420 interest to XYZ Bank. At the same time, Ms Ward pays £180 each month into an investment fund run by an insurance company.

At the end of the 25-year period, Ms Ward hopes that the investment in the fund will have grown sufficiently to repay the £100,000 loan from XYZ Bank and offer an additional lump sum.

The main risks attached to an interest-only mortgage from the borrower's perspective are:

- Borrowers with interest-only mortgages still face the risks that repayment mortgage borrowers face – namely that interest rates may increase and their property is at risk if they fail to keep up the payments to the lender.
- There is also an additional risk that the investment might not grow sufficiently to pay the amount owing on the mortgage. In the example above, there is nothing guaranteeing that, at the end of the 25-year term, the investment in the fund will be worth £100,000 – indeed, it might be worth considerably less.

3.   LIFE ASSURANCE

LEARNING OBJECTIVES

10.3.1   Know the definition of the following types of life policy: term assurance; non-profit; with-profits; unit-linked policies

3.1   Life Assurance

Life assurance is a form of insurance policy where the event insured is a death. Such policies involve the payment of premiums in exchange for life cover – a lump sum that is payable upon death. These life policies are commonly taken out to provide for dependants after death (typically the spouse and children), or associated with a mortgage payment used to pay off the loan on the death of the borrower.

3.2   Term Assurance and Whole-of-Life

There are two kinds of life assurance policy:

- term assurance; and
- whole-of-life.

A term assurance policy is for a set period, say, 25 years. If the policyholder dies during the term then his/her dependants receive the insured sum – if not, then nothing is payable.

The amount of the premiums paid for term assurance will depend on:

- the amount insured;
- age, sex and family history;
- other risk factors, including state of health (for example, whether the individual is a smoker or non-smoker) his occupation and whether he participates in dangerous sports such as hang-gliding; and
- the term over which cover is required.

Policies can be level term, eg, £500,000 cover over the whole 25 years, decreasing term (the amount falls over time – often linked to a repayment mortgage where capital is steadily being repaid during the term) or increasing term (where the cover and premiums rise, for example, with inflation or by a set percentage each year). Policies can pay either a lump sum on death or a regular monthly amount over the remaining term. The latter is known as a 'family income benefit policy'.

Whole-of-life plans are investment-based policies (usually 'with-profits' schemes – see below) which may pay a sum calculated as a guaranteed amount plus any profits made during the period between the policy being taken out and the death of the insured.

The total paid out, therefore, depends on the guaranteed sum, the date of death and the investment performance of the fund.

3.3 Types of Policy

There are three main types of policy:

- non-profit;
- with-profits; and
- unit-linked.

A non-profit policy guarantees to pay a set amount of life cover on the death of the person, regardless of when that might occur. This guarantee means that the policy does not depend on investment growth and as a result, the premiums are often very high.

With-profits policies usually have a minimum amount of life cover which increases each year by the addition of annual bonuses. These bonuses are based on the performance of the underlying investment portfolio and are usually spread out over a number of years to smooth the effect of fluctuating stock market returns. These bonuses permanently increase the basic guaranteed sum.

With unit-linked policies, the premiums are used to buy units in the insurance company's investment fund and part is used to pay for the life assurance cover. The eventual return will instead be dependent upon the performance of the funds selected.

HOTSPOT

10

Go online to your elearning product for further information on life assurance.

If you haven't purchased your elearning product, you can order now by calling Client Services on +44(0)20 7645 0680.

END OF CHAPTER QUESTIONS

Think of an answer for each question and refer to the appropriate section for confirmation.

Question	Answer Reference
1. When can a lender repossess the specific property which was purchased with a loan?	Section 1.1.3
2. How can the interest rates on different types of loans or accounts be readily compared?	Section 1.2
3. Firm A charges interest annually at 6% pa on loans and Firm B charges interest quarterly at 6% pa. Which is the more expensive?	Section 1.2
4. Your firm offers fixed rate loans at 6% pa charged quarterly. Ingoring charges, what is the APR on the loan?	Section 1.2
5. An individual took out a second mortgage through your firm to finance the purchase of a second home in Spain. It was secured on his property in the UK on which he had an existing mortgage through another company. If he is unable to meet his outgoings and his UK property is repossessed, which mortgage will be repaid first?	Section 2.1
6. What are the main differences between the different ways in which interest is calculated on mortgages?	Section 2.1
7. What are the principal risks associated with interest-only mortgages?	Section 2.2.2
8. What is the difference between life insurance and life assurance?	Section 3.1
9. What are the main factors that will influence the premium for a term assurance policy?	Section 3.2
10. What are the key differences between non-profit, with-profit and unit-linked policies?	Section 3.3

GLOSSARY

Active Management

A type of investment approach employed to generate returns in excess of the market.

Alternative Investment Market (AIM)

Established by the London Stock Exchange. It is the junior market for smaller company shares.

Annual Equivalent Rate (AER)

The annualised compound rate of interest applied to a cash deposit. Also known as the Annual Effective Rate.

Annual General Meeting (AGM)

Yearly meeting of shareholders. Mainly used to vote on dividends, appoint directors and approve financial statements.

Approved Persons

Employees in controlled functions must be approved by the FSA.

Articles of Association

The legal document which sets out the internal constitution of a company. Included within the articles will be details of shareholder voting rights and company borrowing powers.

Auction

Sales system used by the Debt Management Office when it issues gilts. Successful applicants pay the price they bid.

Authorisation

Required status under FSMA 2000 for firms that want to provide financial services.

Authorised Corporate Director (ACD)

Fund manager for an OEIC.

Authorised Unit Trust (AUT)

Unit trust which is freely marketable. Authorised by the FSA.

Balance of Payments

A summary of all the transactions between a country and the rest of the world. The difference between a country's imports and exports.

Bank of England

The UK's central bank. Implements economic policy decided by the Treasury and determines interest rates.

Basic Rate (of Income Tax)

Rate of tax charged on income that is below the higher rate tax threshold.

Bearer Securities

Those whose ownership is evidenced by the mere possession of a certificate. Ownership can, therefore, pass from hand to hand without any formalities.

Beneficiaries

The beneficial owners of trust property.

Bid Price

Price at which dealers buy stock. It is also the price quoted by unit trusts that are dual-priced for sales of units.

Bonds

Interest bearing securities which entitle holders to annual interest and repayment at maturity. Commonly issued by both companies and governments.

Bonus Issue

A free issue of shares to existing shareholders. No money is paid. The share price falls pro rata. Also known as a *Capitalisation* or *Scrip Issue*.

Broker/Dealer

Member firm of the Stock Exchange.

CAC 40

Index of the prices of major French company shares.

Call Option

Option giving its buyer the right to buy an asset at an agreed price.

Capital Gains Tax (CGT)

Tax payable by individuals on profit made on the disposal of certain assets.

Capitalisation Issue

See *Bonus Issue*.

Central Bank

Central banks typically have responsibility for setting a nation's or a region's short-term interest rate, controlling the money supply, acting as banker and lender of last resort to the banking system and managing the national debt.

Certificated

Ownership designated by certificate.

Certificates of Deposit (CDs)

Certificates issued by a bank as evidence that interest bearing funds have been deposited with it. CDs are traded within the money market.

City Code (on Takeovers and Mergers)

Rule book developed by the panel on takeovers and mergers to regulate conduct during a takeover.

Clean Price

The quoted price of a gilt. The price quoted for a gilt excludes any interest that has accrued from the last interest payment date and is known as the 'clean' price. Accrued interest is added on afterwards and the price is then known as the 'dirty' price.

Closed-ended

Organisations such as companies which are a fixed size as determined by their share capital. Commonly used to distinguish investments trusts (closed-ended) from unit trusts and OEICs (open-ended).

Closing

Reversing an original position by, for example, selling what you have previously bought.

Commercial Paper (CP)

Money market instrument issued by large corporates.

Commission

Charges for acting as agent or broker.

Committee of European Securities Regulators (CESR)

Represents regulatory bodies from across the EU.

Commodity

Items including sugar, wheat, oil and copper. Derivatives of commodities are traded on exchanges (eg, oil futures on ICE Futures).

Competition Commission (CC)

Government agency that decides whether or not a proposed takeover should be allowed on competition grounds.

Contract

A standard unit of trading in derivatives.

Controlled Functions

Job roles which require the employee to be approved by the FSA. There are five groups of controlled functions.

Convertible Bond

Bond convertible into, at investor's choice, the same company's shares.

Coupon

Amount of interest paid on a bond.

Covered Warrant

A type of option that is traded on a stock exchange.

Credit Creation

Expansion of loans which increases the money supply.

CREST

Electronic settlement system used to hold stock and settle transactions for UK shares.

Data Protection Act 1998

Legislation regulating use of client data.

Debt Management Office (DMO)

Agency responsible for issuing gilts on behalf of the Treasury.

Dematerialised (Form)

System where securities are held electronically without certificates.

Derivatives

Options and futures. Their price is derived from an underlying asset.

Dilution Levy

An additional charge levied on investors buying or selling units in a single priced fund to offset any potential effect that large purchases or sales can have on the value of the fund.

Dirty Price

The price quoted for a gilt excludes any interest that has accrued from the last interest payment date and is known as the 'clean' price. Accrued interest is added on afterwards and the price is then known as the 'dirty' price.

Diversification

Investment strategy of spreading risk by investing in a range of investments.

Dividend

Distribution of profits by a company.

Dividend Yield

Most recent dividend as a percentage of current share price.

Dow Jones Index

Major share index in the USA, based on the prices of 30 major company shares.

Dual Pricing

System in which a unit trust manager quotes two prices at which investors can sell and buy.

Economic and Monetary Union (EMU)

System adopted by most members of the European Union where their individual currencies were abolished and replaced by the euro.

Economic Cycle

The course an economy conventionally takes as economic growth fluctuates over time. Also known as the Business Cycle.

Economic Growth

The growth of GDP or GNP expressed in real terms usually over the course of a calendar year. Often used as a barometer of an economy's health.

Effective Control

Under the City Code on Takeovers and Mergers effective control arises at 30%.

Effective Rate

The annualised compound rate of interest applied to a cash deposit. Also known as the Annual Equivalent Rate (AER).

Equity

Another name for shares. It can also be used to refer to the amount by which the value of a house exceeds any mortgage or borrowings secured on it.

Eurobond

An interest bearing security issued internationally.

Exchange

Marketplace for trading investments.

Exchange Rate

Rate at which one currency can be exchanged for another.

Exchanged-Traded Fund (ETF)

Type of collective investment scheme that is open-ended but traded on an investment exchange, rather than directly with the fund's managers.

Ex-Dividend (xd)

The period during which the purchase of shares or bonds (on which a dividend or coupon payment has been declared) does not entitle the new holder to this next dividend or interest payment.

Exercise an Option

Take up the right to buy or sell the underlying asset in an option.

Exercise Price

The price at which the right conferred by an option can be exercised by the holder against the writer.

Extraordinary General Meeting (EGM)

A company meeting, other than an AGM, at which matters that urgently require a special resolution are put to the company's shareholders.

Financial Services Authority (FSA)

The regulator of the financial services sector created by FSMA 2000.

Financial Services and Markets Act 2000 (FSMA 2000)

Legislation which provides the framework for regulating financial services.

Financial Securities and Markets Tribunal

Judicial body to which firms and individuals can appeal concerning FSA regulatory decisions.

Fiscal Policy

The use of government spending, taxation and borrowing policies to either boost or restrain domestic demand in the economy so as to maintain full employment and price stability.

Fiscal Years

Fiscal years run from 6 April to 5 April. They are the periods of assessment for income tax and capital gains tax.

Fit and Proper

FSMA 2000 requires that every firm conducting financial services business must be 'fit and proper'.

Fixed-Interest Security

A tradable negotiable instrument, issued by a borrower for a fixed term, during which a regular and predetermined fixed rate of interest, based upon a nominal value, is paid to the holder until it is redeemed and the principal is repaid.

Fixed-Rate Borrowing

Borrowing where a set interest rate is paid.

Floating Rate Notes (FRNs)

Debt securities issued with a coupon periodically referenced to a benchmark interest rate.

Forex

Abbreviation for foreign exchange trading.

Forward

A derivatives contract that creates a legally binding obligation between two parties for one to buy and the other to sell a prespecified amount of an asset at a prespecified price on a prespecified future date. As individually negotiated contracts, forwards are not traded on a derivatives exchange.

Forward Exchange Rate

An exchange rate set today, embodied in a forward contract, that will apply to a foreign exchange transaction at some prespecified point in the future.

FTSE 100

Main UK share index of 100 leading shares ('Footsie').

FTSE 250

UK share index based on the 250 shares immediately below the top 100.

FTSE 350

Index combining the FTSE 100 and FTSE 250 indices.

FTSE All Share Index

Index comprising around 98% of UK-listed shares by value.

Full Listing

Those public limited companies (plcs) admitted to the London Stock Exchange's (LSE) official list. Companies seeking a full listing on the LSE must satisfy the UK Listing Authority's (UKLA) stringent listing requirements and continuing obligations once listed.

Fund Manager

Firm that invests money on behalf of customers.

Fund Supermarket

An internet-based service that provides a convenient way of investing in collective investment funds by allowing a variety of funds to be purchased from a number of different management groups in one place.

Future

An agreement to buy or sell an item at a future date, at a price agreed today.

Futures and Options Fund (FOF)

Type of authorised unit trust which invests partially in derivatives.

Gilt-Edged Market Makers (GEMMs)

A firm that is a market maker in gilts.

Gilt-Edged Security

UK government bond.

Gross Domestic Product (GDP)

A measure of a country's output.

Gross Redemption Yield (GRY)

The annual compound return from holding a bond to maturity taking into account both interest payments and any capital gain or loss at maturity.

Harmonised Index of Consumer Prices (HICP)

Standard measurement of inflation throughout the European Union.

Hedging

A technique employed to reduce the impact of adverse price movements in financial assets held.

Higher Rate (of Income Tax)

Tax on top band of income, currently 40%.

Holder

Investor who buys put or call options.

Independent Financial Adviser (IFA)

A financial adviser who is not tied to the products of any one product provider and is duty bound to give clients best advice and offer them the option of paying for advice. IFAs must establish the financial planning needs of their clients through a personal fact find and satisfy these needs with the most appropriate products offered in the marketplace.

Individual Savings Account (ISA)

Savings scheme introduced in 1999 which provides a wrapper in which cash stocks and shares can be held and benefit from tax concessions.

Inflation

An increase in the general level of prices.

Inheritance Tax (IHT)

Tax on the value of an estate when a person dies.

Initial Public Offering (IPO)

A new issue of ordinary shares whether made by an offer for sale, an offer for subscription or a placing. Also known as a new issue.

Insider Dealing

Criminal offence by people with unpublished price-sensitive information who deal, advise others to deal or pass the information on.

Integration

Third stage of money laundering.

IntercontinentalExchange (ICE)

ICE operates regulated global futures exchanges and over-the-counter (OTC) markets for agricultural, energy, equity index and currency contracts, as well as credit derivatives. ICE conducts its energy futures markets through ICE Futures Europe, which is based in London.

In-the-Money

Call option where the exercise price is below current market price (or put option where exercise price is above).

Investment Bank

Business that specialises in raising debt and equity for companies.

Investment Company with Variable Capital (ICVC)

Alternative term for an OEIC.

Investment Trust (Company)

A company, not a trust, which invests in a diversified range of investments.

Irredeemable Gilt

A gilt with no redemption date. Investors receive interest in perpetuity.

Layering

Second stage in money laundering.

LIFFE CONNECT

Order-driven trading system on NYSE Liffe.

Limit Order

SETS order input. If not completed immediately the residual quantity is displayed on the screen as part of the relevant queue.

Liquidity

Ease with which an item can be traded on the market. Liquid markets are described as deep.

Liquidity Risk

The risk that shares may be difficult to sell at a reasonable price.

Listing

Companies whose securities are listed on the London Stock Exchange and available to be traded.

Lloyd's of London

World's largest insurance market.

Loan Stock

A corporate bond issued in the domestic bond market without any underlying collateral, or security.

London Interbank Offered Rate (LIBOR)

A benchmark money market interest rate.

London Metal Exchange (LME)

Market for trading in derivatives of certain metals; such as copper, zinc and aluminium.

London Stock Exchange (LSE)

Main UK market for securities.

Long Position

The position following the purchase of a security or buying a derivative.

Market

All exchanges are markets – electronic or physical meeting place where assets are bought or sold.

Market Capitalisation

Total market value of a company's shares.

Market Maker

An LSE member firm which is obliged to offer to buy and sell securities in which it is registered throughout the mandatory quote period. In return for providing this liquidity to the market, it can make its profits through the differences at which it buys and sells.

Maturity

Date when the capital on a bond is repaid.

Memorandum of Association

The legal document that principally defines a company's powers, or objects, and its relationship with the outside world. The Memorandum also details the number and nominal value of shares the company is authorised to issue and has issued.

Merger

The combining of two or more companies into one new entity.

Mixed Economy

Economy which works through a combination of market forces and government involvement.

Monetary Policy

The setting of short-term interest rates by a central bank in order to manage domestic demand and achieve price stability in the economy.

Monetary Policy Committee (MPC)

Committee run by the Bank of England which sets interest rates.

Mutual Fund

A type of collective investment scheme found in the US.

Names

Participants at Lloyd's of London who form syndicates to write insurance business. Both individuals and companies can be names.

NASDAQ

US market specialising in the shares of technology companies.

NASDAQ Composite

NASDAQ stock index.

National Debt

A government's total outstanding borrowing resulting from financing successive budget deficits, mainly through the issue of government-backed securities.

National Savings and Investments (NS&I)

Government agency that provides investment products for the retail market.

Nikkei 225

Main Japanese share index.

Nominal Value

The amount of a bond that will be repaid on maturity. Also known as face or par value.

Nominated Adviser

Firm which advises AIM companies on their regulatory responsibilities.

NYSE Euronext

European stock exchange network formed by the merger of the Paris, Brussels and Amsterdam exchanges and has since merged with the New York Stock Exchange.

NYSE Liffe

The UK's principal derivatives exchange for trading financial and soft commodity derivatives products. Owned by Euronext.

Offer Price

Price at which dealers sell stock. It is also the price quoted by unit trusts that are dual-priced for purchases of units.

Office of Fair Trading (OFT)

Government agency that refers proposed takeovers to the Competition Commission.

Open

Initiate a transaction, eg, an opening purchase or sale of a future. Normally reversed by a closing transaction.

Open Economy

Country with no restrictions on trading with other countries.

Open-Ended

Type of investment such as OEICs or unit trusts which can expand without limit.

Open-Ended Investment Company (OEIC)

Collective investment vehicle similar to unit trusts. Alternatively described as an ICVC (Investment Company with Variable Capital).

Open-Outcry

Trading system used by some derivatives exchanges. Participants stand on the floor of the exchange and call out transactions they would like to undertake.

Opening

Undertaking a transaction which creates a long or short position.

Option

A derivative giving the buyer the right, but not the obligation, to buy or sell an asset.

Out-of-the-Money

Call option where the exercise or strike price is above the market price or a put option where it is below.

Over-the-Counter (OTC) Derivatives

Derivatives that are not traded on a derivatives exchange, owing to their non-standardised contract specifications.

Panel on Takeovers and Mergers (POTAM or PTM)

A self-regulatory body that produces the City Code regulating takeovers.

Passive Management

An investment approach that aims to track the performance of a stock market index.

Personal Allowance

Amount of income that each person can earn each year tax-free.

Personal Equity Plan (PEP)

Investment scheme in which investors bought shares through a PEP manager. Income and gains are tax-free. New PEPs have not been allowed since April 1999 and existing ones became ISAs from 6 April 2008.

Placement

First stage of money laundering.

Platform

Platforms are online services such as fund supermarkets and wraps that are used by intermediaries to view and administer their investment client's portfolios.

PLUS Markets

PLUS is a stock market based in London and is a competitor to the London Stock Exchange. It has two markets, PLUS traded where securities from across Europe can be traded and PLUS quoted which is a market for small cap shares and is a competitor to AIM.

Pre-Emption Rights

The rights accorded to ordinary shareholders under company law to subscribe for new ordinary shares issued by the company, in which they have the shareholding, for cash before the shares are offered to outside investors.

Preference Share

Shares which pay fixed dividends. Do not have voting rights.

Premium

The amount of cash paid by the holder of an option to the writer in exchange for conferring a right.

Premium Bond

National Savings and Investments bonds that pay prizes each month. Winnings are tax-free.

Primary Market

The function of a stock exchange in bringing securities to the market and raising funds.

Protectionism

The economic policy of restraining trade between countries by imposing methods such as tariffs and quotas on imported goods

Proxy

Appointee who votes on a shareholder's behalf at company meetings.

Public Sector Net Cash Requirement (PSNCR)

Shortfall of government revenue compared to government expenditure.

Put Option

Option where buyer has the right to sell an asset.

Qualifying Corporate Bonds (QCBs)

UK corporate bonds issued in sterling without conversion rights. QCBs are free of capital gains tax (CGT).

Quote-Driven

Dealing system driven by securities firms who quote buying and selling prices.

Real Estate Investment Trust (REIT)

An investment trust that specialises in investing in commercial property.

Redeemable Security

A security issued with a known maturity, or redemption, date.

Redemption

The repayment of Principal to the holder of a redeemable security.

Registrar

An official of a company who maintains the share register.

Repo

The sale and repurchase of bonds between two parties: the repurchase being made at a price and date fixed in advance.

Resolution

Proposal on which shareholders vote.

Retail Bank

Organisation that provides banking facilities to individuals and small/medium businesses.

Retail Prices Index (RPI)

Index that measures the movement of prices.

Rights Issue

The issue of new ordinary shares to a company's shareholders in proportion to each shareholder's existing shareholding, usually at a price deeply discounted to that prevailing in the market.

RPIX

Index that shows the underlying rate of inflation, excluding the impact of mortgage payments.

Scrip Issue

See Bonus Issue.

Secondary Market

Market place for trading in existing securities.

Securities

Bonds and equities.

Settlor

The creator of a trust.

Share Capital

The Nominal Value of a company's Equity or Ordinary Shares. A company's authorised share capital is the Nominal Value of Equity the company may issue while issued share capital is that which the company has issued. The term share capital is often extended to include a company's preference shares.

Short Position

The position following the sale of a security not owned or selling a derivative.

SICAV

Type of European collective investment scheme that is open-ended.

Special Resolution

Proposal put to shareholders requiring 75% of the votes cast.

Spread

Difference between a buying (bid) and selling (ask or offer) price.

Stamp Duty

Tax at ½% on purchase of certain assets.

Stamp Duty Land Tax

Tax charged on the purchase of properties and land above a certain value.

Stamp Duty Reserve Tax (SDRT)

Stamp duty levied at ½% on purchase of dematerialised equities.

State-Controlled Economy

Country where all economic activity is controlled by the state.

Stock Exchange Automated Quotations (SEAQ)

LSE screen display system where market makers display prices at which they are willing to deal. Used mainly for fixed-income stocks and small cap shares.

Stock Exchange Electronic Trading Service (SETS)

LSE's electronic order-driven trading system.

Stock Exchange Electronic Trading Service – quotes and crosses (SETSqx)

SETSqx is a trading platform for securities less liquid than those traded on SETS. It combines a periodic electronic auction book with standalone quote-driven market making.

STRIPS

The principal and interest payments of those designated gilts that can be separately traded as Zero Coupon Bonds (ZCBs). STRIPS is the acronym for Separate Trading of Registered Interest and Principal of Securities.

Swap

An Over-the-Counter (OTC) Derivative whereby two parties exchange a series of periodic payments based on a notional principal amount over an agreed term. Swaps can take the form of interest rate swaps, currency swaps and equity swaps.

Swinging Price

Where a single priced investment fund moves its pricing to a dual priced basis as a result of a large number of buy or sell orders.

Syndicate

Lloyd's names joining together to write insurance.

T + 3

The three-day rolling settlement period over which all deals executed on the London Stock Exchange's (LSE) SETS are settled.

Takeover

When one company buys more than 50% of the shares of another.

Third Party Administrator

A firm that specialises in undertaking investment administration for other firms.

Treasury

Government department ultimately responsible for the regulation of the financial services industry.

Treasury Bills

Short-term (usually 90-day) borrowings of the UK government. Issued at a discount to the nominal value at which they will mature. Traded in the money market.

Trustees

The legal owners of trust property who owe a duty of skill and care to the trust's beneficiaries.

Two-Way Price

Prices quoted by a market maker at which they are willing to buy (bid) and sell (offer).

Underlying

Asset from which a derivative is derived.

Unit Trust

A system whereby money from investors is pooled together and invested collectively on their behalf into an open-ended trust.

Wraps

A type of fund platform that enables advisers to take a holistic view of the various assets that a client has in a variety of accounts.

Writer

Party selling an option. The writers receive premiums in exchange for taking the risk of being exercised against.

Xetra Dax

German shares index, comprising 30 shares.

Yellow Strip

Section on each SEAQ display, showing the most favourable prices.

Yield

Income from an investment as a percentage of the current price.

Yield Curve

The depiction of the relationship between the yields and the maturity of bonds of the same type.

Zero Coupon Bonds (ZCBs)

Bonds issued at a discount to their nominal value that do not pay a coupon but which are redeemed at par on a prespecified future date.

ABBREVIATIONS

ACD	Authorised Corporate Director
AER	Annual Equivalent Rate
AGM	Annual General Meeting
AIM	Alternative Investment Market
APR	Annual Percentage Rate
AUT	Authorised Unit Trust
CBOE	Chicago Board Options Exchange
CC	Competition Commission
CD	Certificate of Deposit
CESR	Committee of European Securities Regulators
CGT	Capital Gains Tax
CP	Commercial Paper
CTF	Child Trust Fund
DCA	Department of Constitutional Affairs
DMO	Debt Management Office
EGM	Extraordinary General Meeting
EMU	Economic and Monetary Union
ETF	Exchange-Traded Fund
EU	European Union
FCP	Fonds Commun de Placement
FOF	Futures and Options Fund
FOS	Financial Ombudsman Service
FSA	Financial Services Authority
FSAP	Financial Securities Action Plan
FSCS	Financial Services Compensation Scheme
FRN	Floating-Rate Note
FSMA	Financial Services and Markets Act (2000)
GDP	Gross Domestic Product
GEMM	Gilt-Edged Market Maker
GRY	Gross Redemption Yield

HICP	Harmonised Index of Consumer Prices
HMRC	Her Majesty's Revenue and Customs
ICVC	Investment Companies with Variable Capital
IHT	Inheritance Tax
ICE	IntercontinentalExchange
IFA	Independent Financial Adviser
IMA	Investment Management Association
IOSCO	International Organisation of Securities Commissions
IPO	Initial Public Offer
ISA	Individual Savings Account
ISD	Investment Services Directive
ITC	Investment Trust Company
JMLSG	Joint Money Laundering Steering Group
LIBOR	London Interbank Offered Rate
LME	London Metal Exchange
LSE	London Stock Exchange
MiFID	Markets in Financial Instruments Directive
MLRO	Money Laundering Reporting Officer
MPC	Monetary Policy Committee
MTS	An electronic exchange for trading European government bonds
NAV	Net Asset Value
NCIS	National Criminal Intelligence Service
NCS	National Crime Squad
NSI	National Savings and Investments
NURS	Non-UCITS Retail Schemes
OEIC	Open-Ended Investment Company
OFT	Office of Fair Trading
OTC	Over-The-Counter
PEP	Personal Equity Plan
PEP	Politically Exposed Person
PLC	Public Limited Company
POCA	Proceeds of Crime Act 2002

POTAM	Panel on Takeovers and Mergers
PSNCR	Public Sector Net Cash Requirement
QCB	Qualifying Corporate Bond
REIT	Real Estate Investment Trust
RPI	Retail Price Index
RPIX	Retail Price Index (excluding mortgages)
S2P	State Second Pension
SSAS	Small Self-Administered Scheme
SDLT	Stamp Duty Land Tax
SDRT	Stamp Duty Reserve Tax
SEAQ	Stock Exchange Automated Quotation system
SETS	Stock Exchange Electronic Trading Service
SICAF	Société D'Investissement à Capital Fixe
SIPP	Self-Invested Personal Pension
SOCA	Serious Organised Crime Agency
STRIPS	Separate Trading of Registered Interest and Principal of Securities
SYSC	Senior Management Arrangements, Systems and Controls
TSE	Tokyo Stock Exchange
UCITS	Undertakings for Collective Investment in Transferable Securities
UKIS	UK Immigration Service
UKLA	United Kingdom Listing Authority
VAT	Value Added Tax
XD	Ex-dividend
ZCB	Zero Coupon Bond

MULTIPLE CHOICE QUESTIONS

The following additional questions have been compiled to reflect as closely as possible the examination standard you will experience in your examination. Please note, however, they are not the CISI examination questions themselves.

Choose one answer for each question. When you have completed all questions, refer to the end of this section for the correct answers.

1. Which ONE of the following is a wholesale market activity associated with an investment bank?
A   Execution-only stockbroking
B   Life assurance
C   Mergers and quisitions
D   Private banking

2. Holding assets in safe-keeping is one of the principal activities of:
A   A custodian bank
B   An international bank
C   An investment bank
D   A retail bank

3. An economy that is characterised by an absence of barriers to trade and controls over foreign exchange is known as:
A   A market economy
B   A mixed economy
C   A state controlled economy
D   An open economy

4. For someone on a fixed income, high levels of inflation would normally:
A   Allow them to save more
B   Reduce their tax allowances
C   Allow them to invest for longer periods
D   Reduce the amount of goods they can buy

5. What is the potential impact of increasing levels of government spending?
A   A decrease in the amount of government bonds issued
B   Falling levels of inflation
C   Reduction in the amount of outstanding government debt
D   Rising levels of inflation

6. How much net interest will be paid to a basic rate tax payer, on a deposit of £10,000 for 6 months at 2.5% pa simple?
A   £125.00
B   £112.50
C   £100.00
D   £75.00

7. Which ONE of the following instruments are zero coupon?
A   Certificates of Deposit
B   Cash ISAs
C   Bank current accounts
D   Treasury Bills

8. Which type of foreign exchange transaction would normally settle two days later?
A   Forward
B   Future
C   Spot
D   Swap

9. Emission contracts are traded on which market?
A   Euronext.Liffe
B   Eurex
C   ICE Futures
D   LME

10. Which one of the following markets would normally trade aluminium and tin derivatives?
A   Euronext.Liffe
B   ICE
C   LME
D   LSE

11. Which world stock market operates on an open outcry basis?
A   Deutsche Borse
B   Euronext
C   NASDAQ
D   NYSE

12. The CAC 40 is an index of which country?
A   England
B   France
C   Germany
D   Japan

13. In the event of a company going into liquidation, who would normally have the lowest priority for payment?
A   Banks
B   Bond holders
C   Ordinary shareholders
D   Preference shareholders

14. What type of corporate action would have taken place if an existing shareholder purchased new shares in the company, thereby increasing the total shares issued?
A   Bonus issue
B   Capitalisation issue
C   Rights issue
D   Scrip Issue

15. The passing of a special resolution at a company meeting requires what MINIMUM percentage of votes in favour?
A   50
B   75
C   90
D   100

16. Which body is responsible for authorising companies to be listed on the London Stock Exchange?
A   Financial Services Authority
B   Office of Fair Trading
C   HR Revenue & Customs
D   Companies House

17. Which ONE of the following is a mandatory corporate action with options?
A   Bonus Issue
B   Merger
C   Rights Issue
D   Takeover

18. Which types of instrument would you expect to see traded on SEAQ?
A   Covered warrants
B   ETFs
C   Fixed income stocks
D   FTSE350 shares

19. 3½% War Stock is an example of which type of UK Government bond?
A   Conventional
B   Dual-dated
C   Index-linked
D   Irredeemable

20. Which type of bond gives the bondholder the right to require the issuer to repay it early?
A   Floating rate note
B   Convertible
C   Medium term note
D   Puttable

21. You have a holding of £10,000 5% Treasury Stock 2014 which is currently priced at 112 and on which you receive half yearly interest of £250. What is its flat yield?
A   5.0%
B   4.46%
C   2.50%
D   2.23%

22. If interest rates increase, what will be the effect on a 5% government bond?
A   Price will rise
B   Price will fall
C   Coupon will rise
D   Coupon will fall

23. Which ONE of the following statements concerning call and put options, is true?
A   The buyer of a call has the right to sell an asset
B   The buyer of a put has the right to buy an asset
C   The seller of a call has the right to sell an asset
D   The buyer of a call has the right to buy an asset

24. An investor who has entered into a contract which commits him to buying the underlying asset at a future date is described as?
A   Holder
B   Long
C   Short
D   Writer

25. Which ONE of the following is always traded as an OTC derivative?
A   Covered warrant
B   Future
C   Option
D   Swap

26. Which type of collective investment scheme (CIS) would you expect to trade at a discount or premium to its net asset value?
A   Unit Trust
B   ETF
C   Investment Trust
D   OEIC

27. Which ONE of the following types of collective investment scheme (CIS) has traditionally been dual priced, but may now also use single pricing?
A ETF
B OEIC
C Investment trust
D Unit trust

28. A fund that aims to mimic the performance of an index deploys which type of investment style?
A Contrarian
B Growth
C Passive
D Momentum

29. An investment fund which can be sold throughout the EU, subject to regulation by its home country regulator is known as:
A An investment trust
B An OEIC
C A SICAV
D A UCITS

30. The standard settlement period for the sale of a unit trust is which of the following?
A T+1
B T+3
C T+4
D T+5

31. What MINIMUM percentage of profits, after expenses, must be distributed for a Real Estate Investment Trust (REIT) to retain its tax status?
A 90
B 85
C 75
D 60

32. What type of investment vehicle makes extensive use of short positions?
A ETF
B Hedge fund
C Passive fund
D OEIC

33. Which, if either, of maintaining confidence in the UK financial system and maintaining the strength of sterling, is a statutory objective of the Financial Services Authority?
A   Both
B   Maintaining confidence in the UK financial system only
C   Maintaining the strength of sterling only
D   Neither

34. A money launderer is actively switching monies between investment products. The stage of money laundering relevant to these activities is known as:
A   Investment
B   Integration
C   Layering
D   Placement

35. The type of Customer Due Diligence necessary when an individual is identified as a Politically Exposed Person (PEP), is known as:
A   Sensitive
B   Enhanced
C   Simplified
D   Non-standard

36. Insider Dealing rules apply to which ONE of the following securities?
A   Commodity derivatives
B   OEIC shares
C   Government bonds
D   Unit trusts

37. What is the MAXIMUM payout that can be awarded by the Financial Ombudsman Service?
A   £30,000
B   £48,000
C   £50,000
D   £100,000

38. Behaviour likely to give a false or misleading impression of the supply, demand or value of the investments deemed under the legislation to be qualifying, is most likely to constitute which ONE of the following offences?
A   Front running
B   Money laundering
C   Market abuse
D   Insider dealing

39. Which ONE of the following assets are exempt from Capital Gains Tax?
A   Buy to let properties
B   Shares
C   UK Government Bonds
D   Unit trusts

40. What additional tax will a higher rate taxpayer with overall income of £100,000 per annum pay on a UK dividend?
A   10%
B   20%
C   22.5%
D   32.5%

41. An investor has subscribed £1,200 to a Stocks & Shares ISA since 6 April 2010. The MAXIMUM amount they can additionally subscribe to the Stocks & Shares ISA in the 2010/2011 tax year is:
A   £3600
B   £6000
C   £7200
D   £9000

42. An investor has subscribed £1200 to a Cash ISA since 6 April 2010. The MAXIMUM amount they can additionally subscribe to the Cash ISA in the 2010/2011 tax year is:
A   £3900
B   £5100
C   £6000
D   £9000

43. What is the MAXIMUM annual amount that can be invested in a Child Trust Fund (CTF), in addition to any Government voucher?
A   £250
B   £1200
C   £3600
D   £7200

44. If an individual investor wishes to be able to manage the investments in a pension themselves, which type of pension would be the most suitable?
A   SSAS
B   SIPP
C   Occupational Pension
D   Stakeholder Pension

45. When an investment bond is encashed, the profits are subject to which tax?
A   Capital Gains Tax
B   Corporation Tax
C   Income Tax
D   Inheritance Tax

46. The individual charged with looking after the assets of a trust is known as the:
A   Beneficiary
B   Executor
C   Settlor
D   Trustee

47. You have a loan where interest is charged quarterly at 12% pa. What is the effective annual rate of borrowing?
A   12%
B   12.18%
C   12.35%
D   12.55%

48. If you expect interest rates to rise over the next few years, which type of mortgage payment would you expect to be most attractive?
A   Tracker
B   Discounted
C   Fixed
D   Variable

49. A policy that only pays out if death occurs during the term of the policy is:
A   An endowment plan
B   A term assurance
C   An income replacement plan
D   A whole-of-life assurance

50. Which ONE of the following types of investment fund is most likely to utilise gearing?
A   ETF
B   Investment trust
C   OEIC
D   Unit trust

ANSWERS TO MULTIPLE CHOICE QUESTION

I. Answer: C   Chapter I, Section 3.3

Advice on mergers and acquisitions is a wholesale market activity provided by investment banks.

2. Answer: A   Chapter I, Section 3.8

The primary role of a Custodian is the safe-keeping of assets.

3. Answer: D   Chapter 2, Section I.4

In an open economy there are few barriers to trade or controls over foreign exchange.

4. Answer: D   Chapter 2, Ref 3.2

High levels of inflation mean that prices rise and so someone on a fixed income would have less money available to buy goods.

5. Answer: D   Chapter 2, Section 4.2.3

Excessive government spending can bring about an increase in inflation.

6. Answer: C   Chapter 3, Section I

Gross interest for the period will be £125 from which £25 tax will be deducted, leaving a net payment of £100.

7. Answer: D   Chapter 3, Section 2

Treasury bills do not pay interest but instead are issued at a discount to par.

8. Answer: C   Chapter 3, Section 4

The 'spot rate' is the rate quoted by a bank for the exchange of one currency for another with immediate effect, however, spot trades are settled two business days after the transaction date.

9. Answer: C   Chapter 3, Section 5.5

ICE operates the electronic global futures and OTC marketplace for trading energy commodity contracts. These contracts include crude oil and refined products, natural gas, power and emissions.

10. Answer: C   Chapter 3, Section 5.6

A range of metals including aluminium, copper, nickel, tin, zinc and lead are traded on the London Metal Exchange (LME).

11.   **Answer: D**   **Chapter 3, Section 6.1.1**

The New York Stock Exchange is the only major exchange to operate on an open outcry basis.

12.   **Answer: B**   **Chapter 3, Section 7.3**

The CAC40 index is used in the French market.

13.   **Answer: C**   **Chapter 4, Section 4.1**

If the company closes down, often described as the company being 'wound up', the ordinary shareholders are paid after everybody else.

14.   **Answer: C**   **Chapter 4, Section 7.1**

Under a rights issue, a shareholder is offered the right to subscribe for further 'new' shares at a fixed price per share.

15.   **Answer: B**   **Chapter 4, Section 2.3**

Matters of major importance, such as a proposed change to the company's constitution, require a 'special resolution' and at least 75% to vote in favour.

16.   **Answer: A**   **Chapter 4, Section 3.2**

The authority responsible is the UK Listing Authority which is part of the FSA.

17.   **Answer: C**   **Chapter 4, Section 7**

A rights issue is a mandatory with options type of corporate action.

18.   **Answer: C**   **Chapter 4, Section 8**

SEAQ is used to trade fixed income stocks and any AIM shares not traded on SETSqx.

19.   **Answer: D**   **Chapter 5, Section 2.4**

3 1/2% War Stock is one of the few examples of an irredeemable stock.

20.   **Answer: D**   **Chapter 5, Section 3.1.2**

Puttable bonds give the bondholder the right to require the issuer to redeem early, on a set date or between specific dates.

21.   **Answer: B**   **Chapter 5, Section 4.2**

The flat yield is calculated by taking the annual coupon and dividing by the bond's price, and then multiplying by 100 to obtain a percentage. So the calculation is 5/112*100 = 4.46%.

22. **Answer: B**   **Chapter 5, Section 4.1**

Bonds have an inverse relationship with interest rates so if interest rates rise, then bond prices will fall.

23. **Answer: D**   **Chapter 6, Section 3.3**

A call option is where the buyer has the right to buy the asset at the exercise price, if he chooses to. The seller is obliged to deliver if the buyer exercises the option.

24. **Answer: B**   **Chapter 6, Section 2.4**

A contract to buy an underlying asset at a future date is a future and the buyer is referred to as long.

25. **Answer: D**   **Chapter 6, Section 4.1**

A swap is a type of OTC derivative.

26. **Answer: C**   **Chapter 7, Section 5**

Investment Trusts are structured and listed on a stock market as with any other type of share and able to borrow money to gear up the portfolio. The share price, however, is not necessarily the same as the value of the underlying investments (determined on a per share basis and referred to as the net asset value). The share price could therefore trade at a premium or discount to the net asset value.

27. **Answer: D**   **Chapter 7, Section 4.1**

Unit trusts have traditionally been dual priced, that is to quote separate prices for buying and selling the units. They now have a choice whether to use dual or simple pricing.

28. **Answer: C**   **Chapter 7, Section 1.2**

A passive fund aims to generate returns in line with a chosen index or benchmark.

29. **Answer: D**   **Chapter 7, Section 1.4.2**

The UCITS directives have been issued with the intention of creating a framework for cross-border sales of investment funds throughout the European Union (EU). They allow an investment fund to be sold throughout the EU subject to regulation by its home country regulator.

30. **Answer: C**   **Chapter 7, Section 4.2**

Fund Groups are required to settle sales within four days of the receipt of all required documentation.

31. **Answer: A**   **Chapter 7, Section 6**

At least 90% of profits, after expenses, must be distributed to shareholders for a REIT to retain its tax status.

32.   Answer: B   Chapter 7, Section 8

Hedge funds have the flexibility to adopt a range of investment styles that can involve the use of short positions.

33.   Answer: B   Chapter 8, Section 1.3

The four statutory objectives of the FSA are maintaining confidence in the UK financial system, reducing the scope for financial crime, promoting the public's awareness of the financial system and ensuring the appropriate degree of protection for consumers.

34.   Answer: C   Chapter 8, Section 2

Layering is the second stage and involves moving the money around in order to make it difficult for the authorities to link the placed funds with the ultimate beneficiary of the money.

35.   Answer: B   Chapter 8, Section 2.2.4

JMLSG guidance requires enhanced due diligence to take account of the greater potential for money laundering in higher risk cases, specifically when the customer is not physically present when being identified, and in respect of PEPs (Politically Exposed Persons) and correspondent banking.

36.   Answer: C   Chapter 8, Section 3

The instruments (securities) covered by the insider dealing legislation in the Criminal Justice Act, includes Government bonds, but does not embrace commodity derivatives, shares in OEICs or unit trusts.

37.   Answer: D   Chapter 8, Section 6.3

The FOS can make an award against that it considers to be fair compensation, however the sum cannot exceed £100,000.

38.   Answer: C   Chapter 8, Section 4

Market abuse includes behaviour likely to give a false or misleading impression of the supply, demand or value of qualifying investments.

39.   Answer: C   Chapter 9, Section 1.2

UK government bolds (gilts) are exempt from CGT.

40.   Answer: C   Chapter 9, Section 1.1

Higher rate taxpayers (overall annual income up to £150,000) are liable to pay tax on dividends at 32.5% but they can offset the tax credit so an additional 22.5% tax is payable.

41. Answer: D   Chapter 9, Section 3.5

There is an annual ISA allowance of £10,200 of which a maximum of £5100 can be invested in a Cash ISA or all can be invested in a Stocks & Shares ISA.

42. Answer: A   Chapter 9, Section 3.5

There is an annual ISA allowance of £10,200 of which a maximum of £5100 can be invested in a Cash ISA. The remaining balance of £3900 can therefore be invested in the Cash ISA.

43. Answer: B   Chapter 9, Section 4

There is an annual limit of £1200 that can be invested in a Child Trust Fund.

44. Answer: B   Chapter 9, Section 5.3

Individuals can manage the investments held within a self-invested personal pension (SIPP) subject to HMRC guidelines.

45. Answer: C   Chapter 9, Section 6

When investment bonds are encashed, the profits made are taxed as income rather than capital gains.

46. Answer: D   Chapter 9, Section 7.1

A settlor creates the trust and the person he gives the property to, to look after for the beneficiaries is the trustee.

47. Answer: D   Chapter 10, Section 1.2

Interest will be charged on the outstanding balance at 3% per quarter so the effective annual rate is $(1.03 \times 1.03 \times 1.03 \times 1.03) - 1 \times 100 = 12.55\%$

48. Answer: C   Chapter 10, Section 2.1

A fixed rate mortgage should be the most attractive if interest rates are expected to rise over the next few years.

49. Answer: B   Chapter 10, Section 3.2

Term Assurance is designed to pay out only if death occurs within a specified period.

50. Answer: B   Chapter 7 , Section 5

One of the distinguishing features of an investment trust is its ability to borrow funds for investment, in other words to use gearing.

INTRODUCTION TO SECURITIES & INVESTMENT/INTRODUCTION TO INVESTMENT

SYLLABUS 10 / WORKBOOK EDITION 26 COMPARISON

Syllabus Unit/Element		Workbook Chapter/Section
ELEMENT 1	INTRODUCTION	
1.1	The Financial Services Industry	
	On completion, the candidate should:	
1.1.1	*know* the role of the following within the financial services industry:	Section 3
	• retail banks	
	• building societies	
	• investment banks	
	• pension funds	
	• insurance companies	
	• fund managers	
	• stockbrokers	
	• custodians	
	• third party administrators (TPAs)	
	• industry trade and professional bodies	
1.1.2	*know* the function of and differences between retail and professional business and who the main customers are in each case:	Section 2
	• retail and professional clients	
1.1.3	*know* the role of the following investment distribution channels:	Section 4
	• independent financial adviser	
	• tied adviser	
	• direct investments	
	• execution only	
ELEMENT 2	ECONOMIC ENVIRONMENT	
2.1	Economic Environment	
	On completion, the candidate should:	
2.1.1	*know* the factors which determine the level of economic activity:	Section 1
	• state-controlled economies	
	• market economies	
	• mixed economies	
	• open economies	
2.1.2	*know* the functions of the Bank of England	Section 2
2.1.3	*know* the functions of the monetary policy committee	Section 2
2.1.4	*know* how goods and services are paid for and how credit is created	Section 3
2.1.5	*understand* the impact of inflation on economic behaviour	Section 3.2
2.1.6	*know* the meaning of the following measures of inflation:	Section 4
	• retail price index	
	• RPIX	
	• consumer price index	
2.1.7	*know* the impact of the following economic data:	Section 4.2
	• Gross Domestic Product (GDP)	
	• balance of payments	
	• Public Sector Net Cash Requirement (PSNCR)	
	• level of unemployment	
ELEMENT 3	FINANCIAL ASSETS AND MARKETS	
3.1	Cash deposits	
	On completion, the candidate should:	
3.1.1	*know* the characteristics of fixed term and instant access deposit accounts	Section 1
3.1.2	*understand* the distinction between gross and net interest payments	Section 1
3.1.3	*be able to calculate* the net interest due given the gross interest rate, the deposited sum, the period and tax rate	Section 1
3.1.4	*know* the advantages and disadvantages of investing in cash	Section

3.2	**Money Market Instruments**	
	On completion, the candidate should:	
3.2.1	*know* the difference between a capital market instrument and a money market instrument	Section 2
3.2.2	*know* the definition and features of the following:	Section 2
	• treasury bill	
	• commercial paper	
	• certificate of deposit	
3.2.3	*know* the advantages and disadvantages of investing in money market instruments	Section 2
3.3	**Property**	
	On completion, the candidate should:	
3.3.1	*know* the characteristics of the property market	Section 3
	• commercial/domestic property	
	• direct/indirect investment	
3.3.2	*know* the advantages and disadvantages of investing in property	Section 3
3.4	**Foreign Exchange Market**	
	On completion, the candidate should:	
3.4.1	*know* the basic structure of the foreign exchange market including spot and forward rates	Section 4
3.5	**Derivatives/Commodity Markets**	
	On completion, the candidate should:	
3.5.1	*know* the characteristics of the derivatives and commodity markets	Section 5
	• trading (metals, energy)	
3.5.2	*know* the advantages and disadvantages of investing in the derivatives and commodity markets	Section 5
3.6	**World Stock Markets**	
	On completion, the candidate should:	
3.6.1	*know* the characteristics of the following exchanges:	
	• London Stock Exchange	Section 6.2.1
	• NYSE	Section 6.1.1
	• NASDAQ	Section 6.1.2
	• Euronext	Section 6.2.2
	• Tokyo Stock Exchange	Section 6.3.1
	• Deutsche Borse	Section 6.2.3
3.6.2	*know* the types and uses of a stock exchange index	Section 7
3.6.3	know the difference between the following London Stock Exchange indices:	Section 7.2
	• FTSE 100	
	• FTSE 250	
	• FTSE 350	
	• FTSE All Share	
3.6.4	*know* to which markets the following indices relate:	Section 7.3
	• Dow Jones Industrial Average	
	• S&P 500	
	• Nikkei 225	
	• CAC40	
	• XETRA Dax	
	• NASDAQ Composite	
ELEMENT 4	**EQUITIES**	
4.1	**Equities**	
	On completion, the candidate should:	
4.1.1	*know* how a company is formed and the differences between private and public companies	Section 2
4.1.2	*know* the features and benefits of ordinary and preference shares:	Sections 4 & 5
	• dividend	
	• capital gain	
	• share benefits	
	• right to subscribe for new shares	

	• right to vote	
4.1.3	*understand* the risks associated with owning shares:	Sections 5
	• price risk	
	• liquidity risk	
	• issuer risk	
4.1.4	*know* the definition of a corporate action and the difference between mandatory, voluntary and mandatory with options	Section 7
4.1.5	*understand* the following terms:	Section 7
	• bonus/scrip/capitalisation issues	
	• rights issues	
	• dividend payments	
	• takeover/merger	
4.1.6	*know* the purpose and format of annual general meetings	Section 2.3
4.1.7	*know* the difference between the primary market and secondary market	Section 3
4.1.8	*know* the main requirements for listing on the London Stock Exchange	Sections 3.2
4.1.9	*know* the advantages and disadvantages of a company obtaining a listing of its shares on the London Stock Exchange	Section 3.1
4.1.10	*know* the role of the Alternative Investment Market (AIM)	Section 3.3
4.1.11	*know* how shares are traded on the London Stock Exchange - SETS/SEAQ/SETSqx	Section 8
4.1.12	*know* the method of holding title – registered v bearer	Section 9
4.1.13	*understand* the role played by Euroclear in the clearing and settlement of equity trades	Section 9.3
	• uncertificated transfers	
	• participants (members, payment banks, registrars)	
ELEMENT 5	**BONDS**	
5.1	**Government Bonds**	
	On completion, the candidate should:	
5.1.1	*know* the definition and features of government bonds	Sections 1, 2
	• DMO maturity classifications	
	• how they are issued	
5.2	**Corporate Bonds**	
	On completion, the candidate should:	
5.2.1	*know* the definitions and features of the following types of bond:	Section 3
	• domestic	
	• foreign	
	• eurobond	
	• asset-backed securities	
	• zero coupon	
	• convertible	
5.3	**Bonds**	
	On completion, the candidate should:	
5.3.1	*know* the advantages and disadvantages of investing in corporate bonds	Section 4
5.3.2	*be able to* calculate the flat yield of a bond	Section 4.2
5.3.3	*understand* the role of credit rating agencies and the differences between investment and non-investment grades	Section 4.3
ELEMENT 6	**DERIVATIVES**	
6.1	**Derivatives Uses**	
	On completion, the candidate should:	
6.1.1	*understand* the uses and application of derivatives	Sections 1, 3, 4
6.2	**Futures**	
	On completion, the candidate should:	
6.2.1	*know* the definition and function of a future	Section 2
6.3	**Options**	
	On completion, the candidate should:	
6.3.1	*know* the definition and function of an option	Section 3
6.3.2	*understand* the following terms:	Section 3
	• calls	
	• puts	

	• covered warrant	
6.4	**TERMINOLOGY**	
	On completion, the candidate should:	
6.4.1	*understand* the following terms:	Section 2
	• long	
	• short	
	• open	
	• close	
	• holder	
	• writing	
	• premium	
	• covered	
	• naked	
	• OTC	
	• exchange-traded	
6.5	**SWAPS**	
	On completion a candidate should:	
6.5.1	*know* the definition and function of an interest rate swap	Section 4
ELEMENT 7	**INVESTMENT FUNDS**	
7.1	**Introduction**	
	On completion, the candidate should:	
7.1.1	*understand* the benefits of collective investment	Section 1.1
7.1.2	*understand* the range of investment strategies – active v passive	Section 1.2
7.1.3	*know* the differences between authorised and unauthorised funds	Section 1.4.1
7.1.4	*know* the purpose and principal features of UCITS	Section 1.4.2
7.1.5	*know* the differences between onshore and offshore funds	Section 1.4.3
7.2	**Unit Trusts**	
	On completion, the candidate should:	
7.2.1	*know* the definition of a unit trust	Section 2
7.2.2	*know* the types of fund and how they are classified	Section 1.3
7.2.3	*know* the roles of the manager and the trustee	Section 2
7.3	**Open Ended Investment Companies (OEICs)**	
	On completion, the candidate should:	
7.3.1	*know* the definition and legal structure of an OEIC	Section 3
7.3.2	*know* the roles of the authorised corporate director and the depositary	Section 3
7.3.3	*know* the terms ICVC, SICAVs and the context in which they are used	Section 3
7.4	**Pricing, Dealing and Settlement**	
7.4.1	*know* how unit trusts and OEICs shares are priced	Section 4
7.4.2	*know* the ways in which charges can be made by the fund manager	Section 4
7.4.3	*know* how shares and units are bought and sold	Section 4.2
7.4.4	*know* how collectives are settled	Section 4.2
7.5	**Investment Trusts**	
	On completion, the candidate should:	
7.5.1	*know* the characteristics of an investment trust:	Section 5
	• share classes	
	• gearing	
7.5.2	*understand* the factors that affect the price of an investment trust	Section 5
7.5.3	*know* the meaning of the discounts and premiums in relation to investment trusts	Section 5
7.5.4	*know* how investment trust shares are traded	Section 5
7.6	**Real Estate Investment Trusts (REITs)**	
	On completion, the candidate should:	
7.6.1	*know* the basics characteristics of REITs:	Section 6
	• tax efficient	
	• property diversification	
	• liquidity	
	• risk	
7.7	**Exchange-Traded Funds**	
	On completion, the candidate should:	
7.7.1	*know* the main characteristics of exchange-traded funds	Section 7

7.7.2	*know* how exchange-traded funds are traded	Section 7
7.8	**Hedge Funds**	
	On completion, the candidate should:	
7.8.1	*know* the basic characteristics of hedge funds:	Section 8
	• risk and risk types	
	• cost and liquidity	
	• investment strategies	
ELEMENT 8	**FINANCIAL SERVICES REGULATION**	
8.1	**Financial Services and Markets Act**	
	On completion, the candidate should:	
8.1.1	*know* the function of the following in the financial services industry:	Section 1
	• regulators (FSA/EC Commission/Committee of European Securities Regulators)	
8.1.2	*understand* the need for regulation and the purpose of the financial services and markets act 2000	Section 1.2
8.1.3	*know* the four statutory objectives of the financial services authority	Section 1.3
8.1.4	*understand* the reasons for authorisation of firms and approved persons	Section 1.4
8.1.5	*understand* the purpose of the FSA's principles-based approach to regulation	Section 1.6
8.1.6	*know* the five groups of activity (controlled functions) requiring approved person status	Section 1.5
8.1.7	*know* the FSA's six outcomes for treating customers fairly	Section 1.6
8.1.8	*know* the role of the financial services and markets tribunal	Section 1.7
8.2	**Financial Crime**	
	On completion, the candidate should:	
8.2.1	*know* what money laundering is and the related criminal offences	Section 2
8.2.2	*know* the purpose and the main provisions of the proceeds of Crime Act 2002 and the money laundering regulations 2007	Sections 2, 2.1
8.2.3	*understand* the three main stages of money laundering	Section 2
8.2.4	*know* the action to be taken by those employed in financial services if money laundering activity is suspected	Sections 2, 2.2
8.2.5	*know* what constitutes satisfactory evidence of identity	Sections 2, 2.2
8.3	**Insider Dealing and Market Abuse**	
	On completion, the candidate should:	
8.3.1	*know* the offences that constitute insider dealing and the instruments covered	Section 3
8.3.2	*know* the offences that constitute market abuse and the instruments covered	Section 4
8.4	**Data Protection Act 1998**	
	On completion, the candidate should:	
8.4.1	*understand* the impact of the Data Protection Act 1998 on firms' activities	Section 5
8.5	**Breaches, Complaints and Compensation**	
	On completion, the candidate should:	
8.5.1	*know* the difference between a breach and a complaint	Section 6.2
8.5.2	*know* the responsibilities of the industry for handling customer complaints and dealing with breaches	Section 6
8.5.3	*know* the role of the Financial Ombudsman Service	Section 6.3
8.5.4	*know* the circumstances under which the financial services compensation scheme pays compensation and the compensation payable for investment claims	Section 6.4
ELEMENT 9	**INVESTMENT WRAPPERS, TAXATION AND TRUSTS**	
9.1	**Tax**	
	On completion, the candidate should:	
9.1.1	*know* the direct and indirect taxes as they apply to individuals:	Section 1
	• income tax	
	• capital gains tax	
	• inheritance tax	
	• stamp duty and stamp duty reserve tax	
	• VAT	

9.1.2	*know* the main exemptions in respect of the main personal taxes	Section 1
9.2	**Individual Savings Accounts (ISAs)**	
	On completion, the candidate should:	
9.2.1	*know* the definition of and aim of ISAs	Section 3
9.2.2	*know* the tax incentives provided by ISAs	Section 3
9.2.3	*know* the types of ISA available	Section 3
9.2.4	*know* the eligibility conditions for investors	Section 3
9.2.5	*know* the following aspects of investing in ISAs	Section 3
	• subscriptions	
	• transfers	
	• withdrawals	
	• number of managers	
	• number of accounts	
9.3	**Child Trust Funds**	
	On completion, the candidate should:	
9.3.1	*know* the tax benefits to a child on the maturity of a child trust fund	Section 4
9.3.2	*know* the main characteristics of child trust funds	Section 4
9.4	**Pensions**	
	On completion, the candidate should:	
9.4.1	*know* the tax incentives provided by pensions	Section 5
9.4.2	*know* the basic characteristics of the following:	Section 5.2
	• state pension scheme	
	• occupational pension schemes	
	• personal pensions including self invested personal pensions (SIPPs)/small self-administered schemes (SSAS)	
	• stakeholder pensions	
9.5	**Investment Bonds**	
	On completion, the candidate should:	
9.5.1	*know* the tax incentives provided by investment bonds – onshore/offshore	Section 6
9.5.2	*know* the main characteristics of investment bonds	Section 6
9.6	**Trusts**	
	On completion, the candidate should:	
9.6.1	*know* the features of the main trusts:	Section 7
	• discretionary	
	• interest in possession	
	• bare	
9.6.2	*know* the definition of the following terms:	Section 7
	• trustee	
	• settlor	
	• beneficiary	
9.6.3	*know* the main reasons for creating trusts	Section 7
ELEMENT 10	**OTHER RETAIL FINANCIAL PRODUCTS**	
10.1	**Loans**	
	On completion, the candidate should:	
10.1.1	*know* the differences between bank loans, overdrafts and credit card borrowing	Section 1
10.1.2	*know* the difference between the quoted interest rate on borrowing and the effective annual rate of borrowing	Section 1.2
10.1.3	*be able to calculate* the effective annual rate of borrowing, given the quoted interest rate and frequency of payment	Section 1.2
10.1.4	*know* the difference between secured and unsecured borrowing	Section 1
10.2	**Mortgages**	
	On completion, the candidate should:	
10.2.1	*understand* the characteristics of the mortgage market:	Section 2
	• interest rates	
10.2.2	*know* the definition of and types of mortgage:	Section 2.2
	• repayment	
	• interest only	
10.3	**Life Assurance**	

	On completion, the candidate should:	
10.3.1	*know* the definition of the following types of life policy:	Section 3
	• term assurance	
	• non-profit	
	• with-profits	
	• unit-linked policies	

Examination Specification

Each examination paper is constructed from a specification that determines the weightings that will be given to each element. The specification is given below.

It is important to note that the numbers quoted may vary slightly from examination to examination as there is some flexibility to ensure that each examination has a consistent level of difficulty. However, the number of questions tested in each element should not change by more than plus or minus 2.

Examination Specification 50 Multiple choice Questions	
Element	**Questions**
1	2
2	3
3	7
4	6
5	4
6	3
7	8
8	6
9	8
10	3
Total	**50**

CISI Membership

Studying for any CISI qualification is certainly not easy, but in view of the current market it will prove to be well worth the effort!

The securities and investments industry attracts ambitious and driven individuals. You're probably one yourself and that's great, but on the other hand you're almost certainly surrounded by lots of other people with similar ambitions. So how can you stay one step ahead during these uncertain times?

Entry Criteria:
- Financial services industry employment
- Suggested study - Introduction to Investment
  IT in Investment Operations

Joining Fee:	None
Annual Subscription (pro rata):	£90
International Annual Subscription:	£67.50

Becoming an Affiliate member of the Chartered Institute for Securities & Investment could well be the next important career move you make this year.

Join our global network of over 40,000 financial services professionals and start enjoying both the professional and personal benefits that CISI membership offers.

(please note that if you are planning on completing the full IAQ, then Associate membership will be more appropriate)

Turn over to find out more about CISI membership

" ... competence is not just about examinations. It is about skills, knowledge, expertise, ethical behaviour and the application and maintenance of all these "

April 2008
FSA, Retail Distribution Review Interim Report

Becoming an Affiliate member of CISI offers you...

- ✓ Use of the CISI CPD Scheme
- ✓ Unlimited free CPD seminars
- ✓ Free access to online training tools including Professional Refresher and Infolink
- ✓ Free webcasts and podcasts
- ✓ Unlimited free attendance at CISI Professional Interest Forums
- ✓ CISI publications including S&I Review and Regulatory Update
- ✓ 30% discount off one CISI conference and one training course
- ✓ Invitation to CISI Annual Lecture
- ✓ Select Benefits — our exclusive personal benefits portfolio

Plus many other networking opportunities which could be invaluable for your career.

To upgrade your student membership to Affiliate,

get in touch...

+44 (0)20 7645 0650
memberservices@cisi.org
cisi.org/membership

CISI Elearning Products

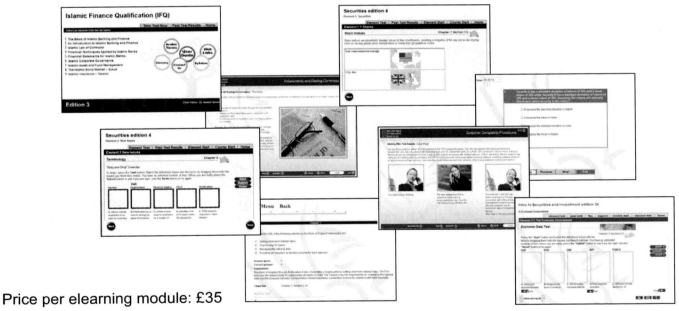

Feedback to CISI

Have you found this workbook to be a valuable aid to your studies? We would like your views, so please email us (learningresources@cisi.org) with any thoughts, ideas or comments.

Accredited Training Providers

Support for examination students studying for the Chartered Institute for Securities & Investment (CISI) Qualifications is provided by several Accredited Training Providers (ATPs), including 7City Learning and BPP. The CISI's ATPs offer a range of face-to-face training courses, distance learning programmes, their own learning resources and study packs which have been accredited by the CISI. The CISI works in close collaboration with its accredited training providers to ensure they are kept informed of changes to CISI examinations so they can build them into their own courses and study packs.

CISI Workbook Specialists Wanted

Workbook Authors

Experienced freelance authors with finance experience, and who have published work in their area of specialism, are sought. Responsibilities include:

*   Updating workbooks in line with new syllabuses and any industry developments
*   Ensuring that the syllabus is fully covered

Workbook Reviewers

Individuals with a high-level knowledge of the subject area are sought. Responsibilities include:

*   Highlighting any inconsistencies against the syllabus
*   Assessing the author's interpretation of the workbook

Workbook Technical Reviewers

Technical reviewers provide a detailed review of the workbook and bring the review comments to the panel. Responsibilities include:

*   Cross-checking the workbook against the syllabus
*   Ensuring sufficient coverage of each learning objective

Workbook Proofreaders

Proofreaders are needed to proof workbooks both grammatically and also in terms of the format and layout. Responsibilities include:

*   Checking for spelling and grammar mistakes
*   Checking for formatting inconsistencies

Notes

Notes

Notes

Notes

Notes

Notes

Notes

Notes

Notes